HAUNTED
LIVERPOOL 8

For Lynne Brown and Louise Cartwright

© Tom Slemen 2003

Published by The Bluecoat Press, Liverpool
Book design by March Design, Liverpool
Printed by The Universities Press, Belfast

ISBN 1 904438 12 1

Tom Slemen
HAUNTED
LIVERPOOL 8

The Bluecoat Press

CONTENTS

INTRODUCTION

In this book I have collected together another selection of strange and intriguing tales about local mysteries and hauntings. In the course of my research into these stories, I came upon many tantalising mysteries which have never been resolved, and they continue to tantalise me. Such is the nature of human curiosity.

I think of such mysteries as the Lion Boy of Jubilee Drive – an unfortunate child who was born with a head of hair that encircled his face like a lion's mane. His facial features were also rather unusual, and added to the likeness of a lion. Many people who lived in Kensington have written to me about the Lion Boy over the years, and several people stated that the child was even mentioned in the *Liverpool Echo* in the early twentieth century. Yet, to date, I have not managed to trace the legendary boy. I'll keep delving, of course, because curiosity in such matters is never satisfied as far as I am concerned.

Another example of a tantalising hint of something that has never been satisfactorily answered, is contained in an intriguing comment made by John Lennon on the evening of Wednesday,11 April 1962. John had recently arrived in Germany to see his friend and former Beatle, Stu Sutcliffe, only to discover that Stu had just died from a brain haemorrhage. John went on stage, but before the performance he made an announcement:

"Stuart Sutcliffe was a very special human being, and a remarkable man. He once told me that he had the ability to see into the future, and I for one now believe that Stu was telling the truth."

What had happened to cause Lennon to say this? We will probably never know, and it continues to vex Beatle biographers to this day.

Whenever I think of the human need to solve a puzzle, I muse on a riddle once posed by Lewis Carroll, the Cheshire-born author of the delightfully surreal *Alice in Wonderland* books. The riddle is: "Why is a writing desk like a raven?" The question is posed by the Mad Hatter, who attends the tea party with Alice, the March Hare and the Dormouse.

"Have you guessed the riddle yet?" the Hatter says, turning to Alice.

"No," says Alice, "I give it up. What is the answer?"

"I haven't the slightest idea," the Hatter tells her.

Readers of the book, however, chose to try and solve the conundrum, even though the Mad Hatter suggests that there is no real answer. They pondered on the question, and many concluded that Carroll had deliberately posed it, knowing that there was an actual answer if you thought long enough. I remember my English teacher at school mentioning the raven and writing desk puzzle. He was just telling us that no one had ever solved it, when a man painting the outside of the school pushed open a window and said, "I know the answer". The teacher folded his arms, and turned to aim a bemused expression at the decorator. "Really?" he asked, with a faint air of condescension.

"Edgar Allan Poe. Poe wrote on them both," said the painter. "He wrote a poem called *The Raven* and he must have written it on a writing desk. So that's the connection between a raven and a writing desk."

"Hmmm, I see – but I doubt it though," said the teacher, sounding like the pompous Captain Mainwaring character out of the *Dad's Army* television series. The painter sulkily resumed his task and closed the classroom window. Everyone in the classroom attempted to solve Carroll's puzzle, but no one came up with anything remotely convincing.

Through sheer curiosity, people will always attempt to solve the riddle, because we all have this inborn need to know things that are unknown. The comedian Dave Allen once remarked how people sometimes watch a ringing telephone for ages, unwilling to answer it because they don't want to speak to anybody, and as soon as the ringing stops, they say, "I wonder who it was?"

Sheer nosiness spurred us to go to the moon, and to discover America, and it's that same inquisitiveness which causes a baby to touch a flame. Inquisitiveness sparked the young Albert Einstein to wonder about the speed of light, and what it would be like to ride on a light beam. I myself have often wondered just why light travels at the speed of 186,281 miles per second. Why that specific six-figured velocity? Through the exploration of such innocent questions, entire edifices of accepted thought have been toppled.

In May 1954, at the age of twenty-five, Roger Bannister ran a mile in under four minutes. It took him three minutes and fifty-nine seconds. Bannister had broken a psychological barrier that had existed since the days of Ancient Greece. He had run a mile in under four minutes; something which many physicians and sportsmen had stated was an impossibility. As soon as Bannister broke through the barrier, others followed closely on his heels. Only forty-six days later, Australian John Landy lowered the record to three minutes and fifty-eight seconds. By 1979 Sebastian Coe had shaved nine seconds off the record, and by the fiftieth anniversary of Bannister's record, over nine hundred and fifty-five men had run a mile in under four minutes.

In 1994 a forty-one-year old man named Eamonn Coghlan beat Bannister's record, and by 2001 Hicham El Guerrouj brought the record down to three minutes and forty-three seconds. Curiosity makes me wonder how long it will be before the three-minute mile becomes a reality, and if there will ever be an ultimate limit to the speed a human can achieve on two legs.

The tales that follow on the pages of this book may leave you asking healthy questions on the nature of life, death, time and space, and our place in the Cosmos. Even the comparatively minor local mysteries I've documented, 'pygmies of triviality' as Sherlock Holmes might call them, might reanimate the childhood sense of magical curiosity that is sadly jaded in so many adults.

Tom Slemen

THE TEACHER CLOCK

I first heard of the strange case of the Teacher Clock from my grandmother when I was a child, and have researched the weird tale over the years to glean the following details.

In Edwardian times, Herbert A Strong, a Professor of Latin, lived in one of the grand old houses in Liverpool's Falkner Square. He was a stern and highly studious academic with a formidable temper. His own children had all grown up and left the family nest, and in the summer months, Professor Strong's eight-year-old niece, Jesamine Middleton, often travelled from her home in Childer Thornton to stay at the house. Unlike Professor Strong's servants, who lived in constant fear of their master's mood swings and fiery temper, the pretty little red-haired girl adored her Uncle Herbert, and he had a soft spot for her as well, although he was usually far too haughty to show his affection openly.

Despite having received an excellent education, Jesamine still had great difficulty reading and speaking certain words, and probably had some form of dyslexia. She said things like 'chimley' instead of chimney, and 'donimo' instead of domino, and had great difficulty remembering and reciting the alphabet in its proper order. The children at school cruelly nicknamed her Muddled-up Middleton and Mixed-up Jesamine and she became increasingly anxious and did not want to go to school.

Aware of Jesamine's learning difficulties, Uncle Herbert attempted to give her intensive private lessons in spoken and written English, but his strong-arm teaching methods only served to put the timid girl on the spot and make her too nervous to learn. His meagre store of patience would quickly be used up and he would slam the chalkboard duster down on the desk and shriek, "Chimney! Chimney! For Mercy's sake, say it, child!"

"Ch ch chim…er…ley," Jesamine would stammer, with her sad face bowed.

Sometimes Jesamine would burst into tears and flee up the stairs to hide inside her aunt's wardrobe. There she would crouch down, amongst her aunt's lavender-smelling finery, with all the hated jumble of letters and unpronounceable words jangling round and round inside her head.

One afternoon, just after she had arrived at her uncle's house and handed her coat to one of the servants, Jesamine was surprised to notice an unfamiliar old grandfather clock towering above her in the hallway. The moment she set eyes upon it, the clock began to chime melodiously, and Jesamine smiled in response. The clock was made of the finest mahogany, with beautiful marquetry panels, and had a very elaborate gold face. She had never seen it before, or at least she had never noticed it.

Filled with curiosity, she opened the door on the front of the clock and watched, mesmerised, as the shining golden pendulum swung slowly to and fro. Her eyes moved from side to side, as they followed the long, heavy pendulum as it slowly and evenly beat time to the clock. The ticking sound seemed to echo around the oak-panelled hallway and as she listened, within the ticking there came a faint voice that spoke the letters of the alphabet, clearly and rhythmically. The voice was that of a softly-spoken woman, and it was very calming and reassuring to Jesamine. In the large, shiny, round weight at the bottom of the swinging pendulum, the face of a smiling old woman gradually appeared, yet the little girl wasn't in the least afraid. The woman's lips moved as she recited the alphabet in a lilting, sing-song voice.

All time seemed to cease while Jesamine stood, transfixed, before the old clock. When a servant came down the hall and gently asked the girl what she was doing, the hypnotic spell was instantly broken. Without thinking, Jesamine rushed into her uncle's study and recited the full alphabet, perfectly, without hesitation. Professor Strong was very impressed at his niece's sudden, and almost miraculous improvement. How had she managed to learn her alphabet in such a short space of time, after so many months of fruitless study? He wanted to know. Jesamine mysteriously replied that the clock in the hall had taught her the alphabet. Uncle Herbert returned a puzzled look to Jesamine, who stood before him bristling with new-found confidence. For once, he managed to hold his tongue and instead of enquiring further, he praised his niece and gave her encouragement, which, in turn, boosted her confidence still further.

Throughout the remainder of that summer, Jesamine would often be found standing spellbound before the old grandfather clock, tracking the pendulum's swing with a look of utter fascination. At school she began to write impressive, well-written and seemingly well-researched tales of kings and battles, of Christopher Columbus and the Great Fire of London – all of which had been told to her by the 'Teacher Clock' as she insisted on calling it. Her grammar improved dramatically, as did her speech and diction, and when her taunting classmates asked Jesamine what her favourite game was, she would eloquently reply, "Dominoes, of course" and wait to see their reaction.

Though delighted by his niece's rapid and unexpected progress, Professor Strong felt unnerved by the tales she told of the Teacher Clock, and her seemingly trance-like behaviour when she stood before it. That grandfather clock had been left to him months before in the will of an old friend – an elderly retired teacher named Mrs Denny, who had died from pneumonia. Had Mrs Denny's spirit somehow become incorporated into the fabric of the old clock? Was it possible that she had returned from beyond the grave to gently teach her last pupil, little Jesamine Middleton?

LIFTING THE VEIL

In 1943 a baby was born in Toxteth, and his mother, on seeing her baby for the first time, became quite concerned because of his strange appearance.

"Louis!" she exclaimed in alarm, calling for her husband. "Look! He's got no eyes!"

The doctor attending the birth looked closely at the infant's face and immediately realised that it was covered with a thin, diaphanous film of skin. He carefully peeled away the film to reveal a pair of tiny, startled blue eyes.

"It's only a caul," said the doctor in a relieved tone. "It's nothing to worry about. In fact, I think they're supposed to bring good luck."

He placed the piece of translucent skin on a table, and after the umbilical cord was cut and the baby was safely snuggled at his mother's breast, the flap of membrane was thrown on to the fire by the child's father, who thought it was rather repulsive. The doctor, having satisfied himself that both mother and baby were doing fine, then packed away all his instruments and bid the new parents good day.

The midwife who had been summoned earlier turned up at the Toxteth house all out of breath and full of apologies, she had been delayed at another delivery and had only just been able to get away. When she heard about the baby being born with a 'veil' she excitedly asked where the skin was. The father then confessed that he had thrown it on the fire. He thought it couldn't possibly be of any use to anyone.

The midwife gazed at the smouldering remains in the grate with a look of anger and frustration. She told the parents that the veils which sometimes covered the face of a newborn baby were highly regarded by sailors, because in maritime folklore, it was said that a seafaring person who carried a veil, or caul, as they were known, could never be drowned. The midwife's husband happened to be a mariner, and she had always wanted a caul to protect him when he was at sea. Despite her profession, this was the nearest she had come to securing a treasured veil for her husband.

Whether or not there is any truth in such beliefs is open to question.

~

At a house in Kirkdale in the 1880s, a set of triplets was born, and each baby had a caul upon its face. In the excitement and confusion after the birth, the young Irish nursemaid, knowing well how highly prized the veils were, stole them from the table upon which the midwife had placed them. She later sold them for a massive one hundred guineas to a relative who was a sea captain. The nursemaid was instantly dismissed when the bizarre theft came to light.

~

During the Second World War, there was a report of a man who was found drifting helplessly in the middle of the North Atlantic, the sole survivor of a German submarine attack upon a Canadian convoy. He wore no life jacket, and was not found clinging to any kind of lifebelt or piece of wreckage, yet he had somehow survived for hours in the treacherous icy conditions of the stormy Northern Atlantic waters.

He was hauled aboard the rescue ship suffering from severe hypothermia and deep shock, but he eventually made a full recovery from his terrible ordeal, although he would be plagued by nightmares for the rest of his life.

When one of his rescuers said that he was lucky to be alive, he strongly disagreed. He explained that his miraculous survival was not simply a matter of luck. He was convinced that it was really down to the fact that the caul of his baby son had been sewn into his belt to prevent him from drowning. All the time he was in the water he had somehow felt safe, protected. He had never seriously felt that he might drown.

Since everyone else in the convoy had perished, he might well have been right.

~

I once met a woman named Jean who had two holes in the upper part of each ear, almost as if her ears had been deliberately pierced at the top. She told me that the puncture marks had actually been left by the removal of a caul that had covered her face at birth. The veil had also left barely visible lines across her forehead and eyebrows.

~

People born with a veil are – according to an ancient superstition – gifted with a special talent, and unusually lucky, but where this belief originated is hard to say.

I know that the wedding veil worn by a bride is supposed to protect her from the 'evil eye', and the only other veil I can associate with the occult, is the veil mentioned in the phrase 'lifting the veil' – which is often used by mediums as they probe into the after-life. In the Old Testament, Moses wore a mysterious veil after talking face to face with God, but why he wore such a covering on his face continues to baffle Biblical scholars.

Certainly the veil has very strong mystical and superstitious associations, whose origins are lost in the mists of time.

THE TRANMERE TERROR

I have studied and investigated ghosts and ghostly encounters for many years, and I have seen from first-hand experience that there are some apparitions that can cause physical or psychological harm. Despite the often-repeated claim that ghosts are not able to harm the living, there are many cases on record of supernatural entities that have inflicted injuries on those unfortunate enough to encounter them.

An unsettling example of a ghost that harmed the living, was the so-called 'Tranmere Terror' – the ghastly apparition of a sinister, gibbering face that terrorised people from Tranmere, Bebington and other parts of Wirral.

The first visitations began in the early 1950s when a night-watchman was sitting at his brazier, in the dead of night, at some roadworks on Church Road, near to St Catherine's Hospital in Tranmere. The time was 3am, when the night-watchman suddenly beheld an evil-looking face that was leering at him out of the blackness as he sat in his box. There was no question that the face was some kind of supernatural presence, surrounded as it was by an aura of fiery, feathery luminescence. Besides, the head had no body underneath it, and it bobbed before him for a while with a hideous, gibbering expression. The night-watchman let out a strangled yelp and felt sick and faint with fear. Fortunately, the flame-lurid face then floated backwards and vanished into the night, leaving the poor man trembling with shock.

Two more night-watchman in other parts of Wirral, encountered the same alarming apparition over the next fortnight, and then the Tranmere Terror, as the press nicknamed him, cast his net wider and began to haunt other members of the public. It was rumoured that one man who had beheld the terrifying face had been so terrified that he had died from heart failure.

A full-blown scare ensued, in which rumour and exaggeration created an atmosphere of pure panic, and the people living in Tranmere and its surrounding areas barricaded themselves into their homes after nightfall. Some believed that the Devil himself was at large in the suburbs of Birkenhead, while others were more sceptical and suspected that a twisted hoaxer was at work. But those who had received a visit from the Terror were not to be fobbed off with such explanations. What they had seen had been no human hoaxer.

One brave man who dared to venture out into the night to track down the dreaded demon was a seventy-two-year-old Liverpudlian named George Garridon. He held a life-long interest in all things supernatural, and he was determined to witness the Tranmere Terror for himself and put an end to all the rumours and speculation. He did not have to wait long. His mission to confront the mysterious bogeyman was accomplished at a street off the Old Chester Road, where the glowing face materialised to terrorise the staff of an old warehouse. Garridon got wind of the incident and rushed to the scene to find people running in all directions from the warehouse in blind panic.

The intrepid pensioner entered the building and saw the Terror drifting towards him across the large abandoned room strewn with boxes which had been abandoned by the fleeing workforce. Instead of joining them, Garridon stood his ground and attempted to communicate with the apparition.

The Terror responded instantly. Orange and scarlet tongues of flame issued from the hovering head, as, in a deep and ominous voice, it spoke several words that were not recognised by Garridon. The pensioner could speak five languages, but could make no sense of the Terror's alien, exotic tongue. The ghost then fell silent and its glowing red eyes seemed full of sorrow before they finally closed, and the head vanished into thin air. Far from being left a trembling wreck, Garridon was delighted that he had at last realised his lifetime's ambition, and come face to face with a real ghost.

The apparition was seen no more after that spectacular confrontation, and the Tranmere Terror remains yet another of Merseyside's unsolved supernatural mysteries.

THE FLYING NUN

The religious Order of Mercy was founded in Ireland on the banks of the River Liffey in 1831, and the nuns belonging to this Order – the Sisters of Mercy – were soon doing their good work in many other parts of the world. One of their convents was built in England in Victorian times in Liverpool's Mount Vernon Street, situated between the Paddington, Low Hill and Kensington areas of the city. By the 1960s, the Mount Vernon Street Convent of Mercy had closed, but by that time the building had acquired quite a supernatural reputation in the local community.

In the early 1960s, two youths from Hall Lane in Low Hill decided to burgle a house on Mount Vernon Street, facing the derelict Convent of Mercy. The house in question was inhabited by an old spinster who was simply known in the neighbourhood as Miss Smith. The youths had chosen their target deliberately – local gossip had it that the elderly woman had all her life savings hidden in the house. Miss Smith was regarded by the people in her neighbourhood as something of an eccentric because she had pictures of the Scared Heart and the Virgin Mary proudly on display in most of her windows. Her front parlour was described by some of her more secularly-minded neighbours, as being like the Vatican, with ornate crucifixes on the walls and statues and relics of the saints and Jesus and Mary cluttered about.

One foggy December evening at around nine o'clock, the two youths, seventeen-year-old Raffy (short for Raphael) and nineteen-year-old Teddy, watched the spinster's house from across the road. Behind them, in the fog, stood the crumbling, twelve foot high wall of the old convent. A dim lightbulb suddenly started to glimmer in the upstairs bedroom of Miss.Smith's house, and after about five minutes, that light went out.

This was the signal that the youths had been waiting for. Raffy scurried across the road and sidled down an alleyway which provided access to the back yard door of the spinster's house. The door was securely bolted, so Raffy quickly scaled the wall and lowered himself noiselessly down into the back yard. He then used nothing more sophisticated than a thin wooden stick from an ice-lolly to insert into a gap in the window frame to knock off the catch.

Whilst all this was going on, Raffy's accomplice, Teddy, was alarmed to see a middle-aged man on a push-bike approaching from the direction of nearby Minshull Street. Teddy quickly put a cigarette in his mouth and cupped his hands around it to partly shield his face. As the cyclist passed by he didn't even glance at Teddy, but instead, he looked up with alarm above where Teddy was standing in the shadow of the wall, at something behind him. With relief, Teddy watched the red light of the bicycle fade into the murky fog, then his attention was drawn back to the front door of Miss Smith's house across the road. It opened slowly to reveal Raffy, who stood there, silently beckoning Teddy. As Teddy was about to enter the spinster's house, Raffy pointed towards the high wall of the former convent across the road.

"Who's that?" he whispered nervously.

Just beyond the top of the wall was the head of a strange figure, which bobbed up and down several times. The two burglars stood uncomfortably in the hallway of the house, not quite sure what they should do next. Who was this strange witness spying on them from the old convent? Next, they saw the figure emerge as far as its waist over the wall, and it became clear that what they were seeing was a nun dressed in a white habit. The two youths had obviously surmised that the woman was standing on some type of platform, or step-ladder, behind that high wall – when she eerily rose right up over the wall until she was suspended in mid-air. After a moment or two hanging, suspended before their eyes, she started to fly through the air across the road towards Raffy and Teddy.

As you can imagine, the sight of the airborne nun zooming towards them sent the two criminals scrambling for cover. Abandoning all thoughts of continuing with the robbery, they rushed through the hall to the back of the house, intending to make an escape down the back alleyway – but when they scuttled out into the back yard, they were confronted by the sight of the ghostly nun standing on top of the back yard wall. Her pallid face seemed as white as her habit, and her sunken eyes were black and lifeless.

At this point, someone let out a scream in the neighbouring yard, as if they too had seen the spooky nun standing on the wall.

The youths turned on their heels and fled back through the house and left via the front door. They ran panting and screaming down Mount Vernon Street with the nun's livid white form hovering close behind them. When they finally reached their homes in Hall Lane, they were relieved to find that the apparition had vanished.

The two youths were convinced that the nun's appearance at the time of the robbery had not been a coincidence. Her behaviour had left them in no doubt that she had made her appearance quite deliberately, to thwart their plan to rob old Miss Smith. Not wishing to provoke a return visit from the ghostly nun, they never went anywhere near the old convent again.

Miss Smith, the old spinster whom the youths had been trying to rob, is thought to have once been a nun herself in her younger years, but no one is quite sure. The identity of the flying nun of Mount Vernon Street remains a mystery, but local people have reported seeing her on many other occasions, floating over the convent wall.

SENTRIES OF STONE

In the school holidays of the blistering summer of 1976, three children from Merseyside went to stay with their relatives in North Wales. They were thirteen-year-old Morgana Phillips from Warbreck Moor in Aintree, fourteen-year-old Roger Fray of Granby Street, Toxteth, and thirteen-year-old Phillip Donnelly from Hoylake. All three were related, and they went to stay with aunties and uncles living near the Whitford area of Flintshire, near Holywell.

The three Merseyside teenagers were made very welcome in Wales and were beside themselves with excitement about what they regarded as an adventure away from their parents. Once they had unpacked all their things and had a snack, they were ready to explore their new surroundings. They were just going out of the door when their aunt stopped them.

"Just before you go, my dears, erm ... there's something I need to tell you."

"OK, we won't talk to any strangers, Auntie Gwen," said Roger. "And if we see the big bad wolf, we'll run back home!" he added sarcastically.

"Very funny! But, seriously, there's a field about a mile away in that direction," Gwen said, pointing in a direction west of the cottage. "Down that lane, across the stream, past the derelict farm to the crossroads. You mustn't go anywhere near it. I don't want to have to tell your parents that you've come to any harm."

"Why, what's going to happen to us if we do?" asked Phillip, trying to sound polite, as he didn't want to upset Auntie Gwen.

"Well, in the middle of the field there's an old, tall, stone cross called the Stone of Lamentations. Nobody from these parts goes anywhere near it. It's said to be protected by very dark forces."

"Oh, come on, Auntie Gwen. You don't really believe in all that rubbish, do you?"

"You can laugh, but I'm not the only one. No one in the village ever goes there any more." Gwen's face remained stern.

"OK, if it makes you happy, we won't go there," said Phillip. "Come on, you two, let's get out of Auntie Gwen's way."

Of course, being the age they were, the minute Gwen had closed the door, the children's appetites for adventure having been whetted, they deliberately set out to find the forbidden field and the Stone of Lamentations. As they ran down the lane they laughed about their Auntie Gwen's 'dark forces' and chased after each other making ghostly noises and shouting, "The dark forces are after you," in exaggerated Welsh accents.

When they reached the crossroads they had little difficulty locating the field. Along two of its sides ran the two roads, at right angles to each other. On the other two sides there was thick forest, which seemed to stretch for miles in both directions. And there, right up in the far corner, was the mediaeval stone cross, and, to their surprise, there seemed to be someone standing by the foot of it.

The mischievous trio suddenly lost all their bravado, but, egged on by each other, they climbed over a stile and made their way up to the cross. By the time they got there, they had all grown completely subdued, and each was secretly wishing that they had taken their aunt's advice and stayed away. There was indeed someone standing by the monument; an elderly, scruffily-dressed man with a huge white beard, leaning very close to the base of the lichen-encrusted cross, apparently trying to decipher the strange symbols and drawings carved into it. At his side was an old grey-nosed Labrador, standing guard over the old man's possessions – various scruffy bundles tied up with string, and a long, faded, green canvas bag. The pair weren't in any way frightening, just rather incongruous in such an isolated spot.

The three curious teenagers gathered around the man, who eventually turned and introduced himself as Mr Hopkins. He then related a marvellous tale that is perfectly true. For as long as people could remember, it was claimed that a very important piece of treasure was buried in the field near to the stone cross. Naturally, over the years, this had brought many people to the field, armed with trowels and spades and, later, metal detectors. Not only had all the treasure seekers failed to find the fabled treasure, many of them had been struck by bolts of lightning in the middle of their labours – even on beautiful summer days when the sky was clear of clouds.

Mr Hopkins admitted that he had also come in search of the treasure, but he was not afraid. He wore a special talisman called the Seal of Solomon, which, he maintained, would prevent him from being struck down, but it would be far from easy. He still had one problem to overcome before he could lay his hands on the legendary treasure. He told them that from the sprawling forest all around the field, ghostly figures on horseback had been seen to ride on certain nights when the moon was full. The figures were said to be dressed in strange armour, and their helmets were horned like the ones reputedly worn by the Vikings. Each of the phantom horsemen was also armed with a bow and arrows. People had reported seeing these apparitions for years, but no one knew whose ghosts they were, or where they came from.

Mr Hopkins said he had studied all of the folklore and obscure history of Wales for many years, and he had come to the conclusion that the ghostly riders were the sentries who guarded the Stone of Lamentations. If just one of their arrows struck a living person, anywhere on the body, that person would drop dead immediately, Hopkins said. The three captivated teenagers shuddered as he said that, even at that moment, he could feel the ancient eyes of the sentries upon him.

"They are watching from the forest right now," he said, looking about him. "They can sense what I am after."

His words filled the youngsters with a sense of foreboding, and they cast nervous glances towards the forest, and instinctively moved closer together. The old man, however, proceeded to bravely pitch his ragged little one-man tent near the forest's edge, while his dog sat, ears pricked, watching and listening. As he worked, puffing and panting with the exertion, Mr Hopkins told the children not to tell anyone he was staying there – he didn't want anybody interfering with his plan.

His tent securely pitched, he squatted down in front of it and consulted an old almanac which confirmed that the moon would be full when it rose. He then produced the long green canvas bag, from which he took a gleaming, polished shotgun. He stroked the barrel of the sleek weapon, which was obviously his pride and joy, and announced that he was going to shoot as many of the ghostly riders as he could, if they chose to put in an appearance that night.

"I read somewhere that ghosts can't be shot," said Morgana. "Are you sure you'll be safe here on your own?"

"Don't you worry, miss," replied Mr Hopkins. "These apparitions are not the usual type of ghost you might meet in a haunted house – they're the product of a long-dead wizard's black magic. The ammunition in this shotgun has been made from a silver crucifix that has been blessed with holy water. The hallowed ammunition will destroy the evil apparitions, and the treasure will no longer then be guarded. You mark my words."

Phillip Donnelly asked just what the treasure was supposed to be, and Mr Hopkins said he believed – from reading and interpreting the arcane drawings on the stone – that it was Merlin's Sceptre; a gilded staff said to have been brought from Atlantis aeons ago. Such staffs, Hopkins stated, had been used to build Stonehenge and the great pyramids in Egypt.

That night, a full moon rose, bathing the landscape in a bright silvery blue that was almost electric, and Hopkins sat before a dying wood fire that glowed with an orange incandescence. His dog, exhausted by the day's events, was curled up next to him. After returning for supper, the three teenagers had managed to slip away from their aunt and uncle's home. Morgana Phillips still wore her pyjamas and slippers.

They sat feeding twigs into the fire's feeble flames. An owl hooted from somewhere in the forest's black depths, followed by a long, strained silence. Then Hopkin's dog suddenly leapt to its feet and let out a long, mournful howl. They heard what sounded like … a horn … then came the rumble of horses' hooves. Morgana and the two boys were terrified, and they took refuge behind the old man – the three of them squashed into the tiny tent.

Hopkins sprang to his feet and took up his position, ready to fire the shotgun. Morgana screamed as the first ghostly figure emerged from the blackness of the forest. It was clad in hefty armour and gave off a faint red glow like St Elmo's Fire. It aimed its bow at Hopkins, but before it could release its deadly arrow, the shotgun discharged its ammunition, and the silver bullet blasted the evil spectre, which vanished instantly along with the black, red-eyed horse.

Two more figures on horseback thundered out from the shadows and the second blast from Hopkins' shotgun caught them both at once and dispatched them to oblivion. While the shotgun was being reloaded, a pale green arrow whizzed within an inch of Roger's knee and hit the Labrador's hind quarters. It yelped just once and fell down dead, yet the arrow vanished the instant it hit the animal.

The shotgun blasted again, and another rider vanished along with its horse. Morgana caught a glimpse of one of the armoured horsemen's faces, and saw that it was not a face at all, but a skull, hideous and with hollow, burning red eyes. The shotgun was discharged again, and the remaining four horsemen pulled up their steeds and turned and rode back from whence they came – deep into the dark depths of the forest. They did not return that night.

At dawn, Hopkins buried his old dog. Roger, Phillip and Morgana went home, sneaking in through the kitchen door and creeping to their beds. Not one of them slept a wink – the awful events of the night playing over and over again in their fevered minds. However, their taste for adventure was undeterred, and they returned to the field at around one in the afternoon only to find the old man sitting by a blazing fire, skinning a rabbit, as calm as could be. Nearby was his sacred ammunition, all packed away ready for the next encounter with the evil sentries on horseback.

After chatting for a while, and marvelling at the old man's survival skills, the three youngsters wandered off into the forest – not too far, and always keeping the field in sight – and there they came upon an amazing find. Lying on the ground was an old horn – about eighteen inches long – elaborately carved out of bone. It had graven spirals and strange Celtic designs etched upon it. The children surmised that one of the sentries must have dropped it the night before, during the chaotic retreat.

Without thinking, Phillip Donnelly picked up the horn, and blew into it. It made a strange low sound that reverberated through the forest. Almost immediately, the ground shook. Then, seemingly out of nowhere, and this time in broad daylight, rode six dark figures on galloping horses. The horn had obviously summoned them. The three of them ran for their lives as a shower of arrows zipped past them. They came crashing out of the forest, startling Mr Hopkins, who was roasting his rabbit on a spit he had fashioned from tree branches. He stood up.

"What's going on?" he asked.

Before any of them could answer, Hopkins heard, then saw, the sentries come hurtling out of the dark green shadows of the forest into the daylight. He hadn't bargained on an attack before nightfall and realised that he wouldn't be able to load his shotgun in time. So he ran. Surprisingly agile for his age, he was running closely behind the fleeing teenagers when there was a loud thud. An arrow had hit him squarely in the back. The old man's body fell instantly and rolled to a halt in the tall grass.

Morgana and the two boys briefly looked back and saw the old man fall. As soon as the horsemen had hit the old man, they had turned and galloped back into the forest, but the youngsters were too frightened for their own lives to go back and look after him. So fast did they run the mile back to their aunt's house, that they had no energy left to speak by the time they reached the cottage.

Gwen got the shock of her life when they burst through the door, and collapsed, gasping, on to the sofa.

"What on earth's the matter with you three?" she asked. "You look like you've seen a ghost."

"Oh, Auntie Gwen, you're not going to believe this," said Roger when he finally summoned enough breath, "but we'll tell you anyway."

The three of them then babbled out their story. Even though it was she who had warned them about the field and the stone cross the day before, for some reason, Gwen could not bring herself to believe their incredible story. When her husband came home, he, too, poured scorn on their story, as did their neighbours on both sides, who treated the rumours which circulated in the neighbourhood as fanciful nonsense.

"City kids!" said one of them. "They see a bit of countryside and go mad. Somebody has been filling their heads with rubbish," she added, giving Gwen a meaningful look.

On the following morning the papers merely stated that an old poacher, who was a bit of a local character, had died of a heart attack and had been found in the field by the crossroads. What made the story more newsworthy was the fact that the grave of his dog had also been found just outside his tent. When the dog's body was disinterred, the vet could find no cause of death.

So it seems that the treasure then, if it exists, is still unclaimed.

This story was related to me by the people who experienced the incredible events at first hand. They are now adults, and they swear that everything in the story really did take place. I have visited the Stone of Lamentations, and also the nearby forest, and although I am not psychic, I had the uncanny sensation that something in the locality was watching me.

People who live in the area also told me of many strange and unnatural deaths that have occurred in the vicinity of the stone over the years, including the freak accident in which a pair of lovers were zapped by a bolt of lightning from a clear blue sky in the 1970s. They survived the strike, but the searing heat caused the skin on the palms of their hands to stick together, as they walked hand in hand. Surgery was required to separate them.

In 1995, an American tourist spotted the stone cross as he approached the crossroads. He was intrigued by its position, in a field, away from all habitation, and he set off to take a closer look. He felt something hard slam into his chest as he was crossing the field, halfway between the stile and the stone cross. With enormous force, the invisible projectile knocked him on to his back, and he subsequently discovered a small round hole in the left breast pocket of his jacket, which had also penetrated his wallet.

TIME AND THE MIND

One morning in the year 2000, at around 3am, I retired to bed. I woke some time later and glanced towards the window to see the pale blue predawn light filtering through the curtains – and it became plain to me that I was not actually in my own bedroom. The window was much larger than my own bedroom window, and it was partly cloaked with heavy, unfamiliar drapes. I then realised that the bed I was lying in was not my bed either. It didn't feel right. The pillows seemed plumper and softer, and the sheets felt different – much crisper, as if they had been starched. I glanced about and confirmed with mounting alarm that I was definitely not in my bedroom, but some other room that seemed to belong to a bygone era; possibly Edwardian or Victorian.

I tried to calm myself, and establish that I was not dreaming. I pinched my arm, and it hurt. I rested my head on the large, sumptuous, feather-filled pillow and closed my eyes tightly. I willed myself back to my own bedroom in the twenty-first century. I visualised my usual bedroom and refused to open my eyes until I could feel the familiar bed and bedclothes around me.

I opened my eyes with some trepidation, and there was the window I knew, with the amber light of a sodium street lamp shining against the curtains. I

·rose from the bed and turned on the light, then had a long think about the strange experience. The day before, I had been theorising to myself on the nature of time, and had come to the intriguing conclusion that the mind, being made of energy, was not limited to the three dimensions of length, breadth and width like ordinary matter. In other words, the mind is not anchored in the dimensions of space like the body, or any other material objects. If pushed, the mind may be able to actually move backwards or forwards along the time dimension – into the past or future.

Well, I had come to deduce that our minds stay in the present because they are 'stuck' there in a rut by our everyday mundane concerns. I decided to meditate on the possibility of inducing the mind to become unstuck from the frame of reference we call the present, and had been meditating upon this for about twenty minutes before going to bed. I am certain that my exercise in psychological time-travel had been a success, yet I didn't repeat the meditation, as I actually feared I might end up marooned in some bygone era.

I know I was not dreaming that morning. The only thing I can't explain is that the experience did not feel psychological. If I had merely dislodged my mind from the year 2000 and pushed it back to say, 1889, then how did I receive real physical sensations during the transferral?

The whole notion of travelling through time fascinates me, and judging from the many letters I receive from readers, the average person in the street is also intrigued by timewarps and timeslips. The following story features an accidental journey through time.

HOUSE HUNTING

In the early 1980s, Suzanne and Julie, a mother and daughter from the Kensington area of Liverpool, were looking for accommodation in the Edge Hill and Wavertree areas of the city. Upon the advice of a relative, Suzanne and Julie went to the offices of Merseyside Improved Houses (MIH) on Wavertree Road, situated between a DIY store and a corner public house known locally as the Royal. The mother and daughter walked up nearby Marmaduke Street and crossed into Wavertree Road, where they located what should have been the MIH building. They entered the premises, and immediately became aware of a distinctive, leathery smell. The interior was dark and rather cold. Suzanne walked up a steep wooden staircase, and her twenty-year-old daughter, Julie, followed closely behind. She felt very nervous as she looked around at the gloomy old room.

At the top of the stairs, the two women came to a poorly-lit landing, and halfway along the landing there was a door. Suzanne opened the door and they approached a counter. Behind the counter hung a dark maroon curtain. The women waited for a while until the curtain was pushed back, and a tall old woman with her grey hair tied up with a bun emerged from behind the gloomy interior of the premises. Suzanne told the woman that they had come to see a housing officer named Miss McGlynn, and the elderly woman returned a slightly baffled look and shook her head. She knew no one of that name. Suzanne then asked about MIH and explained how she and her daughter were hoping to move to a flat in the Edge Hill or Wavertree area. In a strong Lancashire accent, the old woman said she had nothing to do with letting houses, for she was a moneylender. Suzanne apologised, saying that they had obviously come to the wrong place, and she grabbed hold of Julie's arm and ushered her out of the room.

However, leaving the old building was exceedingly difficult, and after negotiating a number of dark corridors and dingy wooden staircases, the mother and daughter were very surprised to find themselves back at the counter where the old moneylender had made her appearance from behind the curtain. However, this time she did not make an appearance, despite their calls for help. This place was coming to feel like the crazy house in Blackpool. In the end, Suzanne and Julie did manage to find their way out of the building on Wavertree Road and went home to Kensington feeling perplexed and frustrated.

They told their story to a relative, who promised to help them find the MIH premises on the following day. With no difficulty, she took them to the modern, well-lit spacious offices of MIH. What is more, on this occasion, there was no trace of the old moneylender's dreary premises, in fact the whole street looked completely different – more modern, brighter.

To this day, Suzanne and Julie still cannot come up with any rational explanation for their disturbing visit to the mysterious building from the past on Wavertree Road.

~

The essence of the mind is made of energy, which has no mass, weight or spatial dimension, and may therefore be capable, under certain circumstances, of transcending the here and now. This leads me on to the intriguing possibility of reincarnation. I remember a boy in my youth named Danny who was black, yet he once divulged to me that he was convinced that he had been born before as a Viking. He had been a black Viking, he claimed, and said he clearly remembered living in a cold, mountainous region. His name had been Kenneth.

One of the history teachers who heard this at my school laughed at the seemingly outlandish claim, and stated that there were certainly no black Vikings. But I never forgot Danny's strange claim, and later researched the history books for any reference to a black Viking. I discovered that there were, in fact, well-established trade routes between Northern Europe and Africa, as well as Asia, India and China. The Norsemen described Africans as 'Blaumenn' – or blue men. One of these Blaumenn, 'Kenneth of Niger', came with the Vikings to Scotland in the tenth century. Was Scotland the cold, mountainous region Danny could remember in his recollections of a possible past life?

A DEAD MAN HANGS

In the early summer of 1977 there were several reports of a figure that was seen running into the River Dee, only to vanish without so much as a splash. A Liverpool family witnessed this strange spectacle, and it was even mentioned on the local Radio City news programme. Perhaps the following story will throw some light on the strange river-bound ghost.

On May Day in 1801, John Clare, a young man in his twenties, put a handkerchief over the lower half of his face and hid in a bush outside a cottage on the outskirts of Chester. Night was falling, and as John Clare gently touched the blade of the knife he was holding, he watched an old woman wearing a bonnet leave her house to travel the short distance to her sister's home, less than half a mile away. It was common knowledge in the neighbourhood that she did this every Friday. The old woman, a Mrs Keel, was said to be an eccentric who practised witchcraft, but what interested John Clare was the fortune in savings that old Mrs Keel was supposed to have secreted under her bed.

As soon as the old woman had tottered off into the gathering dusk, Mr

Clare kicked down the door of the cottage and completely ransacked the place. He crawled right under the bed and felt under every one of the springs. He searched every nook and cranny, but he didn't manage to find anything of value except a few coins in an old vase.

Before leaving the cottage, in a fit of frustration, he started throwing things about. His feelings vented, he started towards the door, but found his way barred by an enormous, black Labrador dog that sat in the doorway and seemed to have appeared out of nowhere. The dog was staring intently at him with a pair of very uncanny-looking eyes. John Clare shouted at the hound, but it didn't even flinch. He was just thinking about climbing out of the cottage by a side window, when he suddenly heard a voice calling out to the dog. It got up and walked away, to reveal old Mrs Keel, standing in the doorway. Her grey, steely eyes stared right through the young burglar, who, having been caught in the act, was now brandishing his knife in panic.

"Get out of my way, old woman, or you'll be done to death," he screamed, hoping to intimidate her.

"I'm a Romany woman," replied Mrs Keel, fixing Clare with her cold eyes, "and by threatening me you have sealed your doom."

John Clare laughed nervously and waved his knife, saying, "Nonsense, get out of my way."

But Mrs Keel gave him the fright of his life when she spoke his name. "John Clare, they will hang you after you kill yourself," she said.

John Clare was puzzled by this weird statement. He decided that he had no alternative; he would now have to kill the old woman, as she somehow knew his name, but just as he lunged towards her, the black dog appeared again with teeth bared, and it chased him out of the house.

The hapless burglar took refuge in the local forest, and intended to leave the Chester area as soon as he could gather together a few possessions, but he was spotted by the sheriff and brought into custody, where Mrs Keel identified him. In 1801, murder was not the only crime that carried the death penalty; people were hanged for burglary and even for stealing loaves of bread. John Clare had not only committed burglary, but had also threatened his victim with a knife. He was sentenced to hang on Saturday 9 May.

As he languished in his cell at the jail, the condemned man hatched a plan. The cart that was to take him to Gallows Hill would stop at a point near the River Dee. Clare planned to make a break for freedom as soon as he was untied in the cart near the gallows. He knew the riverbank well at that point and believed he could lose anyone pursuing him.

On Saturday morning, John Clare had his wrists bound with rope and leg irons were fastened to him at his ankles. He was put in a cart along with two forgers named Thompson and Morgan, and as the cart trundled to the scene of what was billed to be a triple public execution, Clare started smiling, and to the people lining the route hoping to catch a glimpse of the doomed villains, he called out, "They will never hang me, you'll see."

As the cart rumbled on, one of the men forgers was so terrified by the thought of his impending fate, that he was physically sick. The other man started to cry as he realised that he was about to meet his doom, but John Clare simply laughed.

The cart finally rattled to a halt at Gallows Hill, where hundreds of bloodthirsty spectators were waiting to see the three men hang. In those days, a good hanging was something to be eagerly anticipated, a break from the monotony and drudgery of everyday life – a triple hanging was even better. Among the spectators, right at the back of the crowd, stood old Mrs Keel, wearing a large, black hood.

One of the condemned men fainted at the foot of the gallows, and had to be carried up the wooden steps by two laughing men. The other forger was grabbed by the sheriff's men, and he said, "I'm just a forger. I haven't done anybody any real harm. I don't deserve this!"

"You'll just be meat soon," said one of the sheriff's men, pushing him up the steps, which brought chortles of laughter from some members of the mob.

John Clare stood calmly in the cart, awaiting his moment, and eventually his wrists were untied. As soon as his hands were free, he punched the sheriff's man in the face and sent him hurtling off the cart into the crowd. In the confusion, as the mob roared with laughter, John Clare launched himself off the cart, and immediately screamed with pain, because he had forgotten about the heavy leg irons shackled to his ankles. The young man continued with his desperate bid for freedom, but felt as if he was running in slow motion with the irons clamped around his ankles.

The crowd surged after him, and so did the sheriff's men, who found the whole episode hilarious and were now in hysterics. John Clare soon toppled over, and rolled down the steep bank – towards the River Dee. He plunged into the swift-flowing waters, and frantically tried to swim to the opposite bank, but the irons prevented this, and he sank to the bottom and drowned.

Throughout this drama, an old woman in a black hood was cackling with laughter on top of the riverbank as she looked at the terrified face beneath the waters. A wide-eyed, terror-stricken John Clare was looking up at her with the last bubbles of air escaping from his mouth. One hour later, his drowned, livid corpse was recovered from the river, and carried back to the gallows.

With unnecessary cruelty, Thompson and Morgan were made to watch as the limp, dripping body was hanged without the traditional hood on its head. They were then hanged as the crowd of men women and children cheered.

Old Mrs Keel's strange prediction had come to pass – he had indeed been hanged after he had killed himself by jumping into the river.

That night, Mrs Keel was seen standing in the moonlight, surveying the body of John Clare, as it dangled grotesquely from the gibbet. Beside Mrs Keel sat her huge, black, Labrador dog.

DEAD MAN WALKING

To preserve confidential details, the names of the persons mentioned in the following story have been changed.

Arrad Street is an L-shaped back-street that runs from Hope Street to Oxford Street, passing behind a row of houses and the Everyman Theatre. Today it is a lonely, dimly-lit street, but in the 1950s it was even darker, with just a solitary lamp on Oxford Street to illuminate one end of the narrow, cobbled passageway.

At this location in the April of 1956, Arrad Street was the backdrop to a very uncanny event. Before I relate the strange proceedings that took place there, I must go back further in time to the autumn of 1955.

On a November evening of that year, there was an electrifying boxing match at Liverpool Stadium. Liverpool's own middleweight, Billy Ellaway, dazzled the crowds with his onslaught against Guyana-born Kit Pompey. In the audience, a man and a woman sat in their ringside seats, holding hands as they watched the journeymen pugilists engaged in combat. Archie MacIntyre, aged forty-five, and his twenty-one-year-old fiancée, Tina Carney, were rooting for Ellaway, and when the local boxer won the contest on points, the couple went to celebrate the victory at a local pub in St Paul's Square.

At this pub Archie was approached by a man who discreetly took him to one side, and then dropped a bombshell. He said that he had seen Tina with another man, leaving a Lime Street cinema on the previous Sunday. Archie, trying to remain calm, asked Tina for an explanation. Initially she denied that she'd been with another man, but Archie subsequently rummaged through her handbag and discovered a passionately penned love letter, addressed to Tina, and pinned to it was a photograph of an unknown young man.

She broke down and finally confessed to seeing a twenty-nine-year-old man from Cicero Terrace named Larry Thompson. Tina had met him at the Kempston Street factory where she worked, and had been seeing him secretly for about four months. To make matters worse, Tina had recently told Archie that she was pregnant and, as a result, he had obtained a huge loan from a moneylender to finance a lavish wedding.

Now Archie's hopes and dreams lay in tatters, thanks to some punk named Thompson. Archie was renowned for his violent temper, and he swore to his older brother Frank that he would kill Thompson for wrecking his relationship with Tina. Archie had many contacts in Liverpool's underworld, and he soon managed to obtain a gun. Meanwhile, he kept Tina imprisoned inside a locked room in his home and dictated a letter she was forced to write to her secret lover.

With tears in her eyes, the broken-hearted girl wrote the letter and it was posted immediately. Larry received it the next day and read Tina's words. She wanted him to meet her at Arrad Street at the rear of the Hope Hall theatre on Tuesday night at half-past nine. At Archie's insistence, Tina wrote that she thought Archie was having her followed, and Arrad Street was the only place safe enough to meet.

Larry Thompson fell for it all, hook, line and sinker, and arrived at Arrad Street in his car. Archie lurked at the darker end of the street, wearing a pulled-down trilby and a dreary fawn gabardine suit. He watched the headlights of Thompson's car die shortly after the vehicle pulled up near the back of the theatre. Archie nervously felt for the cold metal of the pistol in his coat pocket as he waited.

Eventually, out of the gloom of Arrad Street, came the youthful figure of Larry Thompson. He looked exactly as he looked in the photograph which he'd found in Tina's possession. His rival in love seemed to walk rather unsteadily down the unlit street, until he was about ten feet away. Archie then withdrew the pistol from his coat pocket and aimed it at the figure. Larry threw up his arms defensively with a look of horror on his face, as he stared at the gunman. Archie fired the pistol three times – right at Larry's chest area. The bullets went straight through him and chipped the brickwork of the wall on the left side of the street. Larry clutched his chest and seemed to be in shock. Archie swiftly turned and ran across Hope Street, down Maryland Street, before nipping down South Hunter Street, where his car was parked in an unlit corner.

They say that the criminal always returns to the scene of his crime, and that's exactly what Archie did. After hurling the pistol into the River Mersey at the Pier Head, Archie motored around the night streets for a while, then drove up Oxford Street and slowed down as he passed Arrad Street. He could see Larry Thompson's car, still in the exact same spot where the dead man had parked it. There was no sign of a policeman, or any sort of activity and that baffled Archie.

When he arrived home he broke out into a cold sweat. He was a mess. His brother Frank told him not to worry, as he and five associates would swear in court that they had been playing poker with him at the time of the shooting. He reminded Archie that Tina had been warned that she'd be knifed if she opened her mouth. Archie steadily went to pieces. His hands started to shake uncontrollably and he kept on repeating that he should not have taken a man's life just because he had been betrayed in love. Archie even talked about going to the police station to turn himself in, but Frank reminded him that he'd hang if he did that, and he plied his trembling brother with several glasses of neat scotch to calm his nerves.

In the bedroom upstairs, Tina wailed, knowing that a terrible revenge had been exacted upon her lover.

Frank and Archie sat up all that night expecting a heavy knock at the door, but none came. Every page of the *Liverpool Echo* and other newspapers was scanned by the two men on the following day, but they could find no mention of a murder in Liverpool. Frank asked his younger brother if he was sure he'd hit Larry and Archie said he had definitely blasted him in the chest. It was highly unlikely that any man could have survived being shot in the chest at such close range. Archie said that he even remembered seeing the bullets hit the wall behind Larry, so they could not have been blanks.

That evening, Archie and Frank discovered to their horror that Tina had somehow managed to escape from the room upstairs by climbing out of the window on to a shed in the back yard. The girl dashed to the nearest police station and within minutes, detectives and constables were paying Archie and

31

Frank a visit. The two brothers had no alternative but to open the door to them. The men were quizzed at the police station, and a detective asked Archie why he had kept Tina confined against her will in the bedroom. Archie assumed that Tina had also told the police how she had been forced to write Larry Thompson a letter, luring him to the ambush in Arrad Street. He also presumed that the man's body had been found, so he blurted out his confession to the shooting. "It was a crime of passion," he said, with a tremor in his voice. "I shot Larry Thompson."

The police looked at one another, baffled. Larry Thompson had not been shot. He was certainly dead, there was no question about that, but there was not a scratch upon his body. Naturally, Archie was confused on hearing this. The police said that Larry Thompson had died from a rare heart condition called cardiomyopathy, which often affects young people. He had died in his car just after he had parked it in Arrad Street.

After issuing Archie with a warning never to go near Tina again, the detective angrily added that wasting police time was a serious offence, and he told him to beat it. The detective assumed that Archie had somehow learned of Larry's death, and had then subjected Tina to psychological torture by pretending that he had killed her lover. The letter Tina had written to Larry, asking him to come to Arrad Street was not dated, so the police disregarded it.

Archie later visited Arrad Street with his brother and showed him the three bullet marks in the wall, but there were no signs of any bullets. The brothers left the street, and just before they drove away, Frank broke the silence. He turned to his brother and said, "I wonder if you shot a ghost?" Archie was rather taken aback by the question. Frank hypothesised that perhaps when Larry had died of natural causes in the car, his ghost had left the vehicle in an effort to keep its appointment with Tina, and perhaps it was this apparition that Archie had shot. The bullets had indeed travelled through the ghost's chest and hit the wall behind it, but the ghost – being already dead – could not be killed. Archie had immediately turned and fled, assuming he'd killed a flesh and blood person. Archie remembered that Larry had reflexively thrown up his arms as he opened fire on him. Frank speculated that perhaps at that point Larry had not even realised that he was dead, and had therefore thrown his arms up in fright at the sight of the gun.

The MacIntyre brothers said a prayer for Larry at a church on the way home, and the strange incident caused them to undergo a change of heart which gradually led them to turn their backs on crime.

SLEEPWALKERS

Sleepwalking, or somnambulism, is a sleep disorder which affects an estimated ten per cent of all humans at least once in their lives. Most sleepwalking incidents are of a short duration, but some episodes can last quite a while, and during that time the sleepwalker is at risk of injuring himself or herself. The causes of sleepwalking were once thought to be purely psychological, but some psychiatrists now believe it may be due to other factors, such as a chemical imbalance in the brain, and perhaps as a result of an abnormal reaction to alcohol in the blood. Here are two strange sleepwalking tales.

In 1958, forty-nine-year-old John Williams and his wife Gwen went to stay at the home of his recently widowed Aunt Joan. Joan lived in an old Victorian house in the curved terrace of Sessions Road in Kirkdale. He stayed at the house for a fortnight until his aunt had recovered from the shock of her bereavement, and during that time, some very strange things happened.

Each night, John would have vivid dreams about a beautiful woman from the Victorian age. She wore an elegant bell-bottomed dress of shimmering dark purple satin, and her auburn hair was done up in two elaborate buns on either side of her head. The lucid dreams of this woman were always set in a room that looked exactly like the room John was sleeping in. The only difference was that in the dream, the room had rich velvety wallpaper, wine-coloured curtains, a luxurious-looking four-poster bed, and a dark green carpet. The dreams were always sensual. John would hold the woman closely and kiss her face and neck quite passionately as she sung a lilting song whose lyrics seemed to be French. John and his dream woman would waltz about the room, and the dream would always end when the couple fell on to the four-poster bed. John would always wake up exhausted from the dreams of the dancing lady.

John told his wife Gwen about the dreams, and she had often seen how he would mutter in his sleep, smile, and purse his lips as if he was kissing someone. One morning at four o'clock, a thunderstorm erupted over the skies of Kirkdale, and the loud boom of a thunderbolt shook the house on Sessions Road to its foundations. Gwen awoke with a start, then, seeing that all was well, turned back to snuggle up to her husband – but he wasn't there. She glanced up and saw him waltzing around the room with an invisible partner. The glare of the lightning outside strobed the room, making the weird scene appear even more eerie. Then Gwen noticed that there was something faintly visible waltzing about with her husband. It looked like the barely discernible outline of a woman.

She let out a scream, and her husband immediately collapsed in a heap as the heavens echoed with another crash of thunder. Gwen was so terrified, that she cowered under the blankets and prayed, leaving her husband unconscious on the floor. Then something hard struck her through the blankets. She let out another muffled scream and careered hysterically from the room past something ice cold that brushed past her arm.

When Gwen returned to the room with John's Aunt Joan, they found John lying on his back on the floor with his eyes rolled up into his forehead. He eventually regained consciousness and told them that he had been dreaming of the old-fashioned woman again. He had been waltzing round the room with her, and they had been twirling faster and faster, until ... until ... he couldn't remember anything further.

Gwen flatly refused to sleep in the room that night, and she told John and his aunt that she was convinced that it was haunted. When the couple later returned to their own home in Kirkby, the dreams of the dancing woman stopped at once, and John Williams never walked in his sleep again.

~

An even more terrifying episode concerning sleepwalking and the supernatural took place in the Wavertree area of Liverpool several years ago.

In August 1995, a heatwave swept through Britain, resulting in a drought and with it the usual hose-pipe and sprinkler bans. According to the records, it was the driest period Britain had experienced since 1659. As usual, in such excessive heat, many people had difficulty sleeping. One woman who found the temperature unbearable was Jane, a twenty-five-year-old mother of two who lived in a street off Smithdown Road. Jane's husband Mike was working for a construction firm in London, and was due to return home for the weekend in a few days. Jane and her two children, aged two and four, were missing Mike tremendously, and were looking forward to his return. Jane and Mike had only recently moved into the house, and were planning to buy it from the council when they had saved enough money for a deposit.

On the Sunday night of 13 August 1995, Jane rested naked on the top of her bed, with an oscillating electric fan trained on her. She eventually began to drift off to sleep, and as she did so she experienced a realistic nightmare that left her struggling to wake up. In the terrifying dream, a terrible, fetid stench was evident – the smell of death – and she was standing in the hallway of the house she was now living in. In the dream she was gazing transfixed at an old, white-haired woman with a hunched back. The woman was dressed in a long black gown, and her eyes had a ghastly, penetrating stare. Jane couldn't turn away from her stare, as she was paralysed in the dream, and the evil-looking woman was floating slowly but steadily down the stairs towards her, inch by inch. Jane managed to regain the power of movement, and rushed into the parlour, unable to scream through sheer terror. She expected the woman to come through the doorway into the parlour, as the dreadful stench was getting stronger – but instead, the menacing figure floated through the wall of the parlour with outstretched arms and attempted to throttle her.

At that moment Jane woke from the nightmare drenched in perspiration – and found herself standing up in a dark room. It was the parlour, and she was standing on the very spot where she had been in the nightmare, just before she had awakened. Jane stumbled over an armchair as she groped her way to the wall, feeling for the light switch. She eventually located it and switched on the parlour light. The atmosphere of fear and menace from the nightmare still lingered, and it was some time before Jane was brave enough to walk up the stairs in the hallway where she had first encountered the sinister hunchbacked woman in her dream.

Jane had never walked in her sleep before, and was quite shocked by her unconscious walkabout. She wondered if some hidden anxiety had caused the somnambulism. Perhaps it had something to do with the heat, or the long and lonely nights she had spent yearning for the company of her husband, Jane reasoned. The latter seemed to be the case, because when Mike returned for the weekend from his job down south, Jane enjoyed normal sleep patterns once more. Days later, when he returned to London, the nightmares came flooding back with a vengeance to haunt Jane.

On the Monday night, Jane fell asleep on her sofa, with the television deliberately left on for company. In the dream that formed in her mind, the wizened ghastly face of the old woman in black appeared once more. She kept repeating the words, "Come to me," over and over again, and her dark sinister eyes seemed to possess some strange hypnotic power. Jane could see that the woman was in a cemetery at night, and the only light illuminating the gravestones seemed to be coming from a sodium street lamp. The woman was beckoning Jane, and in the dream she got up off the sofa and left the house. She walked down the night-time street – towards the cemetery.

Jane suddenly awoke with a shock, gasping for breath. She was standing in her bare feet, wearing only her shorts and a vest, and she soon realised that she was in the street outside her home. Not only was she embarrassed to be out in the street in such scanty dress, she found that she had been sleepwalking in the direction of a main road. Across that road was Toxteth Park Cemetery. If she had walked across that road she could so easily have been killed by traffic.

Jane could not face another night in the house without her husband, so she took her children to her mother's house in Gateacre and during the time she stayed there she did not sleepwalk, or experience nightmares.

Not surprisingly, Mike and Jane were put off their new council house by these sinister goings on, and decided not to buy it after all. Jane has since learned from neighbours that the house she had the nightmares in was once inhabited by an eccentric old lady with a hunched back. The woman died in the 1980s and was buried in the local cemetery – just across the road – the one Jane had dreamt about in her sleepwalking nightmare …

TALES FROM THE BLUE LAMP

Many of the stories in my books originate from readers who work very long hours – way outside the usual nine till five. Security guards, milkmen, late-night employees at filling station shops, and police officers, are among those who have related many strange tales to me. Here are several accounts of the supernatural that have been told to me by police officers over the years.

In January 1973, Paul Whitby was a serving police constable who had recently been posted to F Division at Belle Vale Police Station. Paul set off on bicycle patrol duty just after parade, at around 11pm, accompanied by another, older colleague.

The men left the station, walking beside their cycles along Besford Road towards Hartsbourne Avenue through the cold January night. They wore body warmers, gloves, and heavy gabardine coats. Paul was scheduled to split up from the other policeman at the junction of Hartsbourne Avenue and

Childwall Valley Road. As the two officers neared the junction at Well Lane, they came upon a tall man in a long, black, ankle-length overcoat standing at the kerb. His hair was also long and black, but the policemen couldn't make out his facial features clearly, as he was standing side on.

As the policemen drew nearer to the figure they rang their cycle bells to alert him, but he did not turn to acknowledge them, and seemed oblivious to their presence.

"He'd better move out the way. We're not crossing to get out of his way," Paul remarked.

The policemen came within four feet of the man, and still he remained standing there stock-still. Then he suddenly vanished into thin air right before their startled eyes. Paul was naturally frightened by the vanishing act, but his colleague – a religious man who was a lay preacher from the Plymouth Brethren – confidently told him to carry on along the lane and not to look back. The policemen then had to split up to commence their beats. Paul later had to double back and pass the very spot where he had seen the man vanish, but he did not encounter him again. However, he had the distinct, unsettling feeling that the man in black was watching him, unseen.

Around this time in that same area, there was a sect of Satanists who had been desecrating graves at a local churchyard. One body had been exhumed and removed from its coffin, and the police posted officers to keep a graveyard watch on the church. Whether the silent ghost on Well Lane was the disturbed spirit from one of the desecrated graves is unknown.

Later in the 1970s, two policemen in the same area were called out late one night in April to investigate reports of an arsonist who had been seen starting fires near the Wheathill Farm estate, on the immense fields that stretch from Bowring Park and the M62 motorway, to Sarum Road in the Childwall area. The two police constables, Smith and Bacon, left their Panda patrol car on Naylors Road and climbed a fence to gain access to the overgrown field. The time was midnight, and the policemen swept the beams of their torches across the dark fields, searching for the pyromaniac, when they suddenly noticed a dim orange glow in the distance. A yellow fire flared up from the orange light, and the policemen walked steadily towards it, after switching off their torches.

As they neared the blaze, they were very surprised and unsettled by what they saw. They could discern the silhouettes of about thirty naked men and women, holding hands as they walked around a bonfire. The policemen got down on the ground and observed the strange spectacle from behind some clumps of overgrown grass. The people were chanting something unintelligible as they circled the fire in a counter-clockwise direction. One of the policemen suggested radioing for back-up, while the other constable, who regarded the bizarre ceremony as a joke, decided he wanted to take a closer look. He crawled along on his belly, commando-style, until he was close enough to see the faces of the eerie midnight revellers. He stopped in his tracks when he suddenly recognised two of the people around the bonfire. They were two of his next door neighbours from Huyton. For some reason, their familiarity in such a weird setting gave him the creeps, and he decided to beat a hasty retreat.

As he was crawling back through the grass, he knelt on a dry twig. The noise of it snapping brought the naked revellers to a halt and they spotted the two policemen. They chased them across the field wielding hatchets and knives, right up as far as the Wheathill farmstead, where the crowd then retreated back towards the fire. By the time the police back-up had arrived, the mob had disappeared from the field.

The night on which this strange event took place was 30 April – St Walpurgis Night – the traditional night for Satanists and witches practising black magic to hold their rendezvous with the Devil. The neighbours whom the policeman had identified at the bonfire indignantly denied ever having taken part in such a ceremony, even though the constable was absolutely certain that he had seen them that night.

~

From the 1980s up to the present day, a ghostly woman has haunted Lime Street Station. She is what is known as a carnate ghost, which means that she appears to be very real and quite solid – until she chooses to dissolve, or vanish into thin air.

The apparition, nicknamed Joyce, has been seen numerous times over the years by commuters and other travellers using Lime Street station and the underground. She appears as a girl of about twenty-five years of age who begs for money to buy a train ticket home, but as soon as someone takes pity on her and offers her the money, she vanishes.

In the early twenty-first century, Joyce was seen standing outside one of the cafés in the railway station one evening, asking people if they could spare a few pence to enable her to travel home to Huyton. On this occasion, two policemen on point duty noticed the begging girl and approached her, advising her that she was causing an obstruction, as she had gradually moved from her usual position outside the café and was now standing at the top of the escalators that led to the underground.

The girl became very upset and started to shout at the policemen, saying she only wanted to get home. One constable asked her what her name was, and the girl said it was Joyce Whitchurch, a name that sounded familiar to the older policeman who was present. She gave a Huyton address that no longer existed. The flat in question had been demolished in the 1980s, and one of the policemen knew this because he was from that area of Huyton. He therefore told the girl to stop messing about and that she must give them her real address. At this, Joyce sped off with incredible speed and agility towards the women's toilets. The police followed her, and stood guard for some time at the entrance to the toilets, but Joyce did not come out. The toilets were then searched, which didn't take long, and it became obvious that the girl had managed to evade them. As the only exit was via the door, this seemed impossible.

Later, back at the police station, the police related the strange vanishing act of Joyce Whitchurch to the desk sergeant. He listened to their tale and then chillingly informed the officers that they weren't the first people to have encountered the begging girl; she was a ghost who haunted the station for some unknown reason. One of the policemen asked if anyone had tried to trace the ghost's family background through the name she had given – Joyce Whitchurch. The sergeant shrugged his shoulders – he wasn't a man to waste police time chasing after ghosts – there was more than enough to keep him occupied in the real world.

On the following evening, the same two policemen were once again patrolling Lime Street Station – when one of them gazed up at the huge, twelve-foot-wide clock with a look of fascination. There were two words engraved on the clock-face: 'Joyce' and 'Whitchurch'. That clock had been made by JB Joyce & Company of Whitchurch, who started making tower clocks in 1690. Today their clocks can be found in railway stations, the towers of many churches, cathedrals and other prominent buildings, including palaces from Singapore to Kabul.

After eyeing the station clock, the policemen looked at each other, and one of them smiled and said, "A ghost with a sense of humour!"

Joyce still haunts the eateries, platforms and waiting areas of Lime Street Station, and like many ghosts that haunt public spaces in modern times, it has been said that she has even been captured on the omniscient closed-circuit television cameras that keep a constant vigil in the railway station. I wonder what Joyce's real name is? And why is she so sadly earthbound at the station, unable to make the journey home?

~

On the High Street in Wavertree, there is a popular bar called Cuffs which occupies the building that originally housed the old police station.

In the 1970s, local people complained to the police about the strange squealing and frantic barking of dogs at the rear of this building. In an attempt to find out who was causing the nuisance, and to determine whether any animal cruelty was going on, the police followed up the complaints on numerous occasions but could never trace the source of the animal sounds.

Could the ghostly dogs be explained by the fact that decades ago, any stray canines were rounded up and taken to an airtight box which was kept at the back of the police station? Once the animals were inside the box, it was sealed, and they were gassed. People who could no longer afford to keep their dogs and wanted to have them put down, also used to bring them to the police station to be gassed in the box. They were charged a shilling by the police for this grisly service.

~

In the 1960s, at a police station in Liverpool, a police recruit asked the officer in charge of the station if he could visit the court that he had heard was situated within the building, and was duly told that he could. However, the recruit had to go unescorted, as the officer was required to remain on duty in the office to man the telephone and deal with enquiries from the public. An hour later, the recruit returned from his inspection of the court and other parts of the station, saying that he had enjoyed his tour. But he also said something that baffled the station's officer. The young officer mentioned that an older police constable had kindly taken him on the tour of the station. The officer at the desk became curious, and he asked the recruit what the collar number of this older constable had been. "It was PC95F," the recruit replied.

Police Constable 95F had recently died of a heart attack whilst on duty in the police station – in fact, while he was in the station's courtroom. The recruit had to accept that he had been escorted round the police station by the dead officer's ghost, and was very shaken by the incident. He failed to complete his probationary period and left the station shortly afterwards.

~

In the 1990s, two policemen on a night patrol in the Woolton area decided to have their break, so they drove their squad car up Speke Road, close to St Julie's High School. The time was almost three in the morning. The driver steered the car up a small narrow driveway which led to the grounds of the elegant Woolton Hall, which was erected in the early years of the eighteenth century, and was once owned by Richard Molyneux of the famous Croxteth Molyneux family in 1704.

Once the police car was parked on the driveway, the policemen sat back in their seats and relaxed. One of them wound down his window and lit a cigarette, while the other unscrewed a thermos flask and poured himself a cup of coffee. The two men had been sitting in silence enjoying their break for a few minutes – when they heard footsteps approaching.

Walking up the driveway, towards the main entrance of Woolton Hall, were two figures. As they passed the parked police car, the constables could see that the man and woman, from the looks of their attire, obviously belonged to a bygone age. The woman wore a long, silken, brocade dress, trimmed with lace in festooned flounces, and a small hat was perched upon her curly head. The man, who had long curly black hair, wore a long embroidered jacket with pagoda sleeves, and below the calf-length coat, a pair of broad-toed boots with spurs was visible. The figures sauntered up to the portico of Woolton Hall and vanished as they passed behind the pillars.

The driver of the police car switched on the vehicle's headlamps and drove slowly towards the entrance. He and his colleague could plainly see that the doors of Woolton Hall were firmly closed, and there were no lights on in the building. The man and woman were nowhere to be seen.

The car reversed at speed back down the long driveway, and was soon heading back along Speke Road at rather more than the legal speed limit!

THE MAIDEN IN THE TOWER

I have written about timeslips before in my books, and the subject evidently fascinates my readers as much as it fascinates me, if the many emails and letters I receive are anything to go by. One of the most intriguing timeslip cases I have been researching is of a Liverpool man named Arthur Davies.

In the late 1930s, young unemployed people were strongly advised to sign up for a government training scheme designed to allow those who were out of work to go on to obtain employment. A propaganda film called *On the Way to Work* was widely shown to induce young people to give the scheme a try. The film featured idyllic rustic scenes of cloth-capped youngsters picking strawberries, making hay, chopping trees and damning streams.

One of the thousands of young men who were naïve enough to swallow the film's rather misleading view of country life was Arthur Davies, a twenty-year-old from Liverpool. Full of optimism, he signed off the dole and was taken to Presteigne in Mid-Wales, where he soon discovered the harsh reality behind the film's rosy promises. He'd become an inmate of what would later be known as a British Slave Camp, where unemployed people were 'reconditioned' to make them fit for the employment market. The taskmasters were ex-soldiers, who ran the camps with the strictest military discipline.

Arthur and the other recruits were awakened by a bugle call each morning at five. After the compulsory ritual salute to the Union Jack, they washed and shaved, consumed a meagre oatmeal breakfast, then took up a pick or shovel and worked for twelve hours. The weekly wage was just two shillings and a packet of Woodbine cigarettes. The labour camp Arthur was in was in a very remote part of Wales – the nearest pub was over twelve miles away – so he had little chance of enjoying his paltry wages.

Under the unbearable July sun, Arthur and the men of the camp were felling trees, hedging, ditching, and carrying out many other laborious tasks, when he noticed something glimmering from a nearby wood. At first he thought it was some mischievous local child reflecting the sun with a mirror to taunt the workers, and during his break, Arthur sneaked over to the wood, determined to catch the mischief-maker.

Upon entering a clearing, Arthur came across a magnificent sight, which left him wondering if he was dreaming. A huge stone castle stood on the far side of the woodland, on a rise. The turrets, battlements and drawbridge of the walled fortress were clearly visible above the treetops. Arthur turned to shout to a friend to come and join him, but he couldn't see anyone in the labour camp. He gazed back at the castle and couldn't resist walking through the wood to get a better view of the mysterious fortifications. A strange white flag fluttered above one of the towers, and far below, the still, green waters of the moat surrounded the castle walls.

A dazzling light suddenly flashed towards Arthur's, and it came from a figure leaning over a parapet on the castle keep. He squinted, and shielded his eyes with his hand. He could just distinguish that the figure was female, with long hair, and she seemed to be signalling to him with some kind of mirror. Arthur was suddenly overwhelmed with a deep feeling of sympathy towards the woman at the top of the tower, almost as if he knew her. He felt an urge to rescue her, and was ready to ascend the hill, when he heard voices behind him. He turned and saw two overseers from the camp advancing towards him. He didn't know what to do. He felt strongly drawn to the woman in the tower, but he knew that he would be in big trouble if he did not get back to work. Shirking, in any form, was not tolerated.

Arthur gazed back towards the castle in an agony of indecision – only to find that it was gone. The guards took hold of the youth, who had tears in his eyes, and escorted him back to the camp, giving him a severe warning about his behaviour as they did so.

Arthur told no one but his sister about the strange mirage, and for decades -- right up until his death in 1972 – he regularly returned to that spot in Wales, in the hope of getting just one more glimpse of the elusive castle and the mysterious damsel who seemed to be a prisoner in its tower.

THE ANSWER BOX

In June 1963, Chris Keaton, a young lad from the Northwood area of Kirkby, went to stay with his Aunt Gladys on Netherfield Road in Everton for a week.

Aunt Gladys was a widow and always made a great fuss of her young nephew, as she had no children of her own. When he arrived, she told him to go and look in the wardrobe in her bedroom. There was something there for him.

Chris rushed into the room and mooched about for a while. He returned empty-handed with a puzzled look on his face. Gladys shook her head in dismay and went to look in the wardrobe herself. She immediately saw that Chris had accidentally pulled down her prized mink coat, which lay in a heap at the bottom of the wardrobe. She never wore it – it had been given to her by an old relative – but she loved the feel of its luxurious silky fur. She picked it up and said sarcastically, "It's under this old thing!" The sarcasm was totally lost on the boy; all he could think about was the surprise which his aunt had in store for him. With a nod and a wink, Gladys then pointed to an old hatbox at the bottom of the wardrobe.

"It's in there," she said. "Go on. Open it."

With a broad smile, Chris picked up the hatbox and opened it. Inside was a large black cowboy hat and a toy silver Colt Forty-Five gun – plus a box of caps. Within minutes, Chris had the hat on and was twirling the gun in his hand like a Western gunslinger. Gladys had to struggle not to laugh at the serious expression on her nephew's face. With an innocence that she found endearing, Chris asked if she knew that Kirkby was really called Dodge City, and he was the Kirkby Kid. Chris then challenged his own shadow to a draw, which was followed by a volley of caps. The cat scuttled behind the sofa, and cowered there until it was sure the noisy young intruder had gone out.

Chris was galloping his imaginary horse down Netherfield Road later that afternoon, still wearing his cowboy hat, when he saw someone that today's children would probably laugh at or ignore, but Chris's heart somersaulted. It was the ragman, pushing his old wooden cart, a limp yellow balloon trailing behind, shouting, "Rags! Any old Rags?" in a sing-song voice, which sent all the local children running excitedly into their houses and emerging shortly afterwards clutching handfuls of old clothes.

Chris remembered what his aunt had said about that old fur coat in the wardrobe – "this old thing", she had said. The boy turned and ran back home to fetch it. Maybe he could get a goldfish for his auntie in return. Aunt Gladys was at Mrs Prendegast's house enjoying her daily gossip. Chris grabbed the mink coat and made a beeline for the ragman, who quickly took it off his hands – a little too quickly. In return, Chris was given a purple party horn. He blew into it, and it unfurled a paper spiral that tapered to an orange feather.

"I want more than that!" Chris demanded, cheekily. "That there's me auntie's mink coat."

After a lot of grumbling, the ragman searched his pockets, then rummaged through the rags on his cart and eventually produced a small green plastic box which he handed to Chris.

"What is it?" the child asked.

"It's an Answer Box. Ask it any question and it will truthfully tell you the answer, but it can only answer yes or no."

Before Chris could ask any further questions, a voice echoing in the distance caught his attention. It was Aunt Gladys, and she wasn't happy.

"Christopher! Christopher! Come here at once. What have you done with my mink coat?"

Whenever an adult called him by his full name he knew it meant trouble and it stopped him in his tracks. By the time he had turned back again, the ragman's cart had trundled off down a side street and away, leaving a street full of children, each clutching a balloon, a whistle, or some other cheap toy.

Within seconds, Gladys had grabbed hold of Chris's collar and was marching him back home.

"That's it!" said Gladys. "You can stay in for the rest of the afternoon. I'm surprised at you, Christopher. I really am."

However, Gladys could not stay angry with him for long and after half an hour back at the house, they were chatting over a cup of tea. Chris decided that it would now be safe to show his aunt the box which the ragman had given him. Rather like Jack from the fairytale showing his mother the handful of beans he had received in exchange for her prize cow, Chris showed Gladys the Answer Box and told her it could answer any question.

"Oh! Pull the other one, you little rascal," said Gladys shaking her head. "I should box your ears, never mind playing with a silly plastic box."

Christopher, however, was unabashed. He was too busy examining the green box and particularly a little plunger button on the top. When he pressed it, the black pointer swung between the words 'Yes' and 'No'. Despite herself, Aunt Gladys seemed equally fascinated by the box, and she asked it, jokingly, "Will I marry a film star?" and then pressed the little button. A spring-loaded mechanism clicked, and the needle immediately swung to the word 'No'.

Chris giggled and he took hold of the box.

"Will Auntie Gladys marry at all?" he asked, then pressed the button.

The box gave its unexpected answer: 'Yes'.

Gladys grinned. She'd lost her husband five years back, and had never really bothered seeing any man since. She did have an admirer, though – a man who lived across the road called Alan – although he was quite a few years younger than she was.

Gladys asked, "Will the man I marry be called Alan?"

The box said, 'No'.

"Wonder who it will be, Auntie?" said Chris, and he innocently quizzed the box with a series of further questions. "Will it be Father O'Hare?"

"Oh! Chris! You little monkey!" smiled Gladys, as the pointer on the box turned to 'No'.

45

"Will it be the coal man?"

'No.'

Gladys was pretending to treat the whole thing as a laugh, yet she was childishly fascinated.

Chris kept questioning the box, "Will it be the milkman?"

'No.'

"Will it be the club man?" Gladys half-joked.

Chris repeated the question. "Will it be the club man?"

'Yes,' came the answer from the box.

A big smile broke out on Chris's face.

Gladys was stunned.

"Auntie, you're going to marry the club man!" said Chris and, as an afterthought, he asked if she'd be having a big wedding cake. "You've got to have a big wedding cake, everybody does."

That week soon flew over, and Chris was back in his Kirkby home. He excitedly showed his dad the Answer Box, and told him about the dozens of answers it had already given. His dad laughed at first, but then he started to wonder as he gazed at the green box. He picked up the newspaper and turned to the racing section, and named each horse running in the 6.30 at Kempton, asking the box if it would win. When he reached a horse called Lovely Money, the box indicated 'Yes'. For every other runner it had read 'No'. Lester Pigott was riding on Lovely Money, which had odds of nine to two.

Chris's Dad couldn't resist giving the box a try. He put money on the horse and it won. "Was this just a coincidence?" he thought. The next horse – named Golden Plume – was also selected by the green box. It too won at odds of seven to one in the nine o'clock meeting at Kempton. And the next horse apparently chosen by the box also won.

Alan saw a change in his father which he didn't like. He wasn't content with his winnings, which were far more than he had ever won before. Instead, he wanted more and more. He talked about going through the pools coupon next, in an attempt to hit the jackpot. That night, when he was drunk, Chris's dad brought two friends around – Joey and Bobby – to show them the box. They laughed at his claims, but became deadly serious when he suddenly said, "Are you seeing another woman, Bobby?"

The box said 'Yes.'

Bobby went crimson and said, "Course I am – the missus."

Chris's dad could see his friend's discomfort but still continued, "Is Bobby seeing another woman besides his wife?"

'Yes,' said the box.

This was true, Bobby was also seeing his neighbour's wife.

To distract Chris's father, and without really knowing where the question came from, Bobby quickly asked, "Will Joey live to reach the age of fifty?"

The pointer quickly swung to 'No.'

"Will Bobby ever reach the age of fifty?" Chris's dad asked.

"Hey! Shut up, will you? I don't want to know," said Bobby, becoming increasingly nervous.

'No,' said the box.

Bobby and Joe were both aged forty-nine at the time. Bobby suddenly erupted and knocked the Answer Box out of Chris's hand and it hit the floor. Something cracked inside it.

"Look what you've done!" cried Chris. "That's my special box that the ragman gave me."

He picked up the box and it rattled. When he pressed the button, the needle refused to move. A fight broke out between Bobby and Chris's dad, and during the altercation, Joey picked the box up and threw it on to the back of the open coal fire. The green plastic soon melted, and as a series of green blobs dripped on to the burning coals, the inside of the box was revealed; nothing more magical than a few small springs and cogs.

A week before their fiftieth birthdays, Bobby and Joey died together in a car crash in Shrewsbury. Chris's Aunt Gladys did end up going out with the club man, and she married him two years later.

Chris believes that the ragman – who was never seen again in the neighbourhood – was actually the Devil.

Perhaps it was all pure coincidence, or the result of Chris's faulty recollections of his childhood. However, to this day, Chris is adamant that the Answer Box which was given to him by the ragman, was able to accurately predict future events, as sinister as they may have been.

CUPID'S SHOT

This story and the following one – A Dangerous Experiment – are both derived from the *Liverpool Albion, The Times,* and several books on Edwardian experiments in anaesthesia. The two accounts are concerned with the misuse of chemicals in an attempt to procure those precious things which money cannot buy.

One of the closely-guarded secrets of the ages is a potion that can make a person fall in love. This potion is not an aphrodisiac. An aphrodisiac – named after Aphrodite, the Greek goddess of sexual love and beauty – is a concoction used to cause lust or desire to develop in a person. If you want to make a person fall in love, you must forget oysters, powdered rhino horn, Spanish Fly, ginseng and zinc supplements, because those things merely create sexual desire. Love, as most people realise, is quite a separate thing altogether, and the ancients created their potions to engender love in a person by extracting certain chemicals from the poppy plant – and also from the flower universally associated with love – the red rose.

Many years ago, in the late 1880s, there was a pharmacy on Lord Street that employed an eccentric chemist named Connel McConnicky. McConnicky had been a pharmacist in Dublin, but had been sacked for creating a variety of concoctions with dangerous side effects. One of his best-sellers was a green tonic called McConnicky's Old Thought Provoker, which was a mild hallucinogenic tonic. But by far the most requested under-the-counter product which McConnicky made was his legendary 'love potion', which he called Cupid's Shot. It was almost prohibitively expensive, retailing at two guineas for a tiny red-tinted bottle of the product, which was to be taken orally. Only the very rich could afford the concoction.

One Spring morning in 1882, Robert Montague, a dishonest businessman from the Cotton Exchange, sidled into the chemist's and discreetly waited until the shop was devoid of customers, before whispering to McConnicky that a friend had recommended Cupid's Shot. He slipped the two golden guineas into the chemist's outstretched palm. McConnicky stooped and reached for the under-the-counter 'medicine'. The tiny red bottle was rapidly wrapped in soft tissue paper and Montague slipped it into his inside coat pocket. After the sale was made, McConnicky gave him the simple instructions: "Pour the entire contents into a beverage which the lady is about to drink, and her heart will open like a rose." McConnicky explained that if the lady had the slightest feeling towards him, she would soon be smothering him with love and affection.

Mr Montague tilted his bowler hat and bade the unscrupulous chemist good morning. He dashed to the old Adelphi Hotel on Ranelagh Place, where he had arranged to have morning coffee with a beautiful young woman named Helena Yeoman. Helena was the nineteen-year-old daughter of Bernard Yeoman, a local entrepreneur who owned a vast empire of jewellery shops in Lancashire and Cheshire. Robert Montague had coldly calculated that if he were to wed Helena, he'd be marrying into enormous wealth. He didn't have any feelings for the girl, but looked upon her solely as an unprecedented business opportunity. Robert had managed to coax Helena into meeting him at the Adelphi hotel, where he was currently staying.

Helena sat in the lounge; a portrait of youthful beauty, and a waitress named Juliette stood nearby, paying her an unusual amount of attention, because she also knew who Helena Yeoman's father was, having once worked at Helena's Aigburth home for two years as a maid.

Robert bowed low and ostentatiously kissed the girl's knuckle. As he sat down at the table, he was apologising profusely because he was several minutes late. Helena forgave him and said that she had been enjoying a conversation with Juliette, the waitress. Coffee was ordered, and Juliette quickly brought it to the table. Robert was making polite conversation, when all of a sudden, a tall, handsome man in a top hat and the finest clothes, entered the lounge. He called Helena's name at the top of his voice and brushed past Robert, who was several years his senior, to embrace her.

The man was Eustace Buncey, an accomplished all-rounder in the sporting world, as well as being one of the most eligible bachelors of his day. Eustace spent a good half-hour at the table in the lounge, paying compliments to the lovely Helena, before finally taking his leave. Robert Montague seethed with envy and resentment as Buncey bragged about several estates he owned in South Africa that had been bequeathed to him by his late uncle.

Rid of the dashing young braggart at last, Robert Montague wondered how he could accomplish the task of emptying the little red bottle into Helena's coffee without her noticing. Even if he did manage to drug the coffee, she might not drink it anyway. It was an expensive risk he had to take. Perhaps he should ask her to close her eyes, and pretend he had a surprise for her, and use the opportunity to pour the potion into the coffee.

As Robert Montague was still working out how to slip the drug into Helena's drink, she left the table after asking to be excused – to powder her nose. Juliette, the waitress, escorted her to the ladies' powder room. Robert looked shiftily about, reached into his pocket, then lurched forward and poured the contents of the red bottle into Helena's cup. He waited patiently for her return, trying not to show his impatience.

Helena eventually made her reappearance, and she immediately smiled at Robert, then began to take delicate sips of the coffee. Juliette stood a few steps behind Robert, waiting upon the couple. The minutes rolled by as Robert Montague steered his conversation from flat anecdotes about his colleagues at the Cotton Exchange, to the depth and unusual blueness of Helena's eyes. Those eyes suddenly looked heavily glazed. She started to breathe deeply, and she placed her hands over her bosom and smiled. It was a loving smile. She reached out towards Robert, and he reached back to her, but Helena roughly brushed his hands aside. Instead, she got up and headed straight for the waitress, Juliette, who was astonished by the sudden attention, yet smiling. The couple embraced and kissed one another passionately. The *Liverpool Albion* describes this, at the time, outrageous display of affection as a 'mania' brought on by the drug.

The red-faced Robert Montague protested meekly, but to no avail – the two women were inseparable from that moment and barely listened to his protestations. After several moments the embarrassed businessman meekly left the hotel, and fearing prosecution for administering the Cupid's Shot drug, boarded a train to Birmingham, where he laid low for a while.

Strange rumours spread that Helena and Juliette underwent a secret type of marriage service soon afterwards. They certainly lived happily together for seventeen years in North Wales. And Robert Montague had to look elsewhere to make his fortune.

A Dangerous Experiment

This story is also concerned with the misuse of a drug for selfish gain. In this case, it was not the abuse of a potion to kindle love, but over-indulgence in a dangerous mind-expanding drink that caused two egotistical men to become gibbering idiots.

The scene for this parable is Rodney Street, in Edwardian Times. In this Liverpudlian equivalent of Harley Street, at Number 78, was the practice of George Arthur Williams, a Harvard-educated dental surgeon. He was a man who also had a wide knowledge of anaesthesia. Williams had a cousin in Mexico who collected various plants with medicinal properties and dispatched them to him. Williams wrote several tracts on the coca plant from which the drug cocaine is derived.

In 1886, John Pemberton had introduced the popular drink Coca-Cola to consumers in America. Amongst other ingredients, the drink contained cocaine, syrup and caffeine. In 1901, the cocaine was removed from the soft drink, because it was thought to be addiction-forming.

As far back as 3000 BC, coca chewing was practised throughout South America to stave off hunger and give extra energy, and the plant was regarded as a gift from God. The Incas cultivated large coca plantations that were later taken over by the Spanish invaders.

George Arthur Williams researched other less-known plants of medicinal value, such as the peyote cactus, which contains a chemical that transforms sounds entering the ear into a kaleidoscope of colours in the brain. Williams experimented with the cactus extract, but found it was of little use in the annulment of pain from tooth nerves. Williams also dabbled with Huanta, a toxic plant from Ecuador with white blossoms, which has the reputation of being the main ingredient in the so-called 'Sorcerer's Drink' which caused shamans to fall into a coma for three days at a time, until they awakened imbued with supernatural wisdom. When Williams drank the diluted juice of the plant, he ended up with nothing more than a lingering headache.

However, the one plant that did seem to hold great potential for the creation of a new pain-killing compound, was a tropical American vine called Yage (pronounced ya-hay). This plant had acquired something of a legendary status in Europe, but obtaining it was exceedingly difficult, as it was mainly found in Amazonia. Williams received a parcel one morning from his cousin across the Atlantic. It was a coil of Yage vine measuring just thirty-six inches in length, sent from Belem in South America. Williams took down a huge, leather-bound volume on the exotic flora of the South American Continent and flipped through the pages until he came upon the section that documented the Yage plant and its use in various controversial preparations.

In order to extract the vital ingredient of the plant, a portion of the vine was to be boiled in distilled water for fourteen hours until it was reduced to a residue. The residue had to be further treated until its essence had been isolated. This distilled spirit then had to be rediluted by infusing it into wine made from the noha grape. The noha grape was banned in France in the 1970s by the French Ministry of Agriculture because the wine it produces is thought to cause insanity through the release of a chemical similar to an hallucinogen found in marijuana.

After several months, two bottles of the Yage wine were produced by Williams and stored in the cellars of 78 Rodney Street. Meanwhile, he devoured as much information on Yage as possible, and even travelled to the reading rooms of the British Library in London to read up on the plant, which was classified under the Latin name of *banisteriopsis caapi*. Williams read various accounts of the effects which Yage wine had on a person once it had been imbibed. Most people who had drunk the wine afterwards told how they had been confronted by terrifying, realistic monsters which did not seem to be Yage-induced hallucinations at all. Had they been drug-induced figments of the mind, the appearance and behaviour of the horrifying phantasms should have varied from person to person, but this was not the case. The people who perceived the monsters always described them in exactly the same way.

There were three species of these monsters: grotesque, gargoyle-like beings; globular black octopuses with squirming tentacles; and an enormous black cat, reminiscent of a panther. The Ecuadorian shamans maintained that these creatures could only be repelled by strong willpower. A weak-minded person would be attacked by the entities, and would either die, or return to the real world with an insane mind. Once the creatures had been 'tamed', the person who had absorbed the Yage wine would be capable of receiving a 'cosmic wisdom' and of even communicating with the dead. The most hazardous part of the entire experiment hinged on consuming exactly the right quantity of wine. Too much, and it would result in incurable madness.

George Arthur Williams wrestled with the pros and cons of personally experimenting with the dangerous brew, and many times he took one of the unlabelled dark purple bottles of Yage wine from the cool cellar and gazed at it. He would repeatedly touch the cork and feel an almost overpowering urge to reach for the corkscrew. But he wasn't ready yet. What if the stories of the monsters from another reality were true?

At a gentlemen's club in Liverpool in May 1906, Williams was smoking his pipe as he stared out of the window into the evening sky. He was contemplating the possibility of using a guinea pig upon which to test the potent wine, when two acquaintances approached him and disturbed his reverie. They were the tall, broad-shouldered Saxon Hill, a successful stockbroker from St Michael's-in-the-Hamlet, and his friend Thomas Canning, a wealthy confectioner who had sold numerous cake recipe books to hotels across Europe. Williams talked to them about the dangerous wine, and the two men responded with sceptical smirks.

Saxon Hill bragged that he was immune to intoxication, and told a rambling story of how he had remained standing after a drinking spree that lasted twelve hours. Each of his other drinking companions finished up lying prostrate on the floor, and one drinker had almost died of alcohol poisoning.

Canning declared that he had never heard of Williams' Yage wine, despite the fact that he was one of the greatest wine connoisseurs in England. Hill lit a huge, ostentatious Havana cigar and offered himself as the ideal guinea pig the American dentist was looking for. Williams instantly took up his offer, but only on the condition that he would not be sued if the wine 'tilted' Hill's brain. Hill promised that he would get a solicitor to draw up a legal document that would exculpate Williams from any responsibility, should the wine incur any damage to his mental health. The stockbroker seemed excited at the possibility of trying the mystical wine, but Canning predicted that the proposed experiment would come to nothing. The confectioner said that he had once inhaled nitrous oxide in his youth because a medical student friend had sworn that the gas provided instant enlightenment. All it had done was make Canning giggle and feel as if he was caught between waking and sleeping.

On the evening of Monday 7 May 1906, Saxon Hill and Thomas Canning arrived together at 78 Rodney Street, and were admitted by a servant and shown into the drawing room, where a bottle of purple Yage wine stood in the centre of a small mahogany table on a silver salver. Next to the bottle was a crystal wine glass and a corkscrew fashioned from a piece of horn. Williams entered the room, and a smiling Saxon Hill handed him the legal document which guaranteed that no action would be taken against him, should the experiment end tragically. As Williams perused the document, Canning drew Hill's attention to an upright wooden chair which was swathed in thick leather straps. Williams explained that Hill would be put in that chair and restrained, in case he became violently hysterical as a reaction to the Yage. Most people in their right minds would have fled on seeing the chair, but the indomitable Hill seemed to be relishing the drama of the situation.

Saxon Hill inserted the corkscrew into the bottle as Williams warned him to be very careful. Williams began to have serious doubts about the experiment, not for Hill's sake, but for his own reputation. If the wine produced no effect, the American would be ridiculed for ever more. He was still wondering whether it was wise to proceed, when, all of a sudden, he felt a sharp nagging pain in his abdomen. The pain was so severe it winded him and made him double up. He had suffered from the same stomach pains at breakfast, and he feared it might be the return of what the doctors had diagnosed as a rumbling appendicitis. The pain receded for a while, and Williams sat at the table, breathing deeply, with his hand over his navel. Saxon Hill poured the wine into a glass, held it up to the bright gas mantle, then sniffed it. "Smells quite sweet," he said.

"Just sip it, Mr Hill," cautioned Williams.

But the foolhardy Hill ostentatiously threw back his head and downed the entire glass.

"No!" wailed Williams, all the time thinking about all the literature he had read which warned about the dosage of the Yage and noha grape concoction.

"I say, calm down, man," said Hill, licking his lips. "The drink hasn't been invented which can damage my iron constitution!"

Williams took out his fob watch and removed the cover to inspect the dial. The time was 7.35pm. According to all the literature he had read, Yage took ten minutes to enter the bloodstream via the stomach wall.

As those ten minutes elapsed, Saxon Hill repeatedly pronounced that he felt as right as rain, and expressed disappointment with Williams who had promised such great things of the drink. At this point, having watched Hill down the wine with no obvious ill effects, Canning's curiosity got the better of him and he picked up the wine bottle, sniffed it's mouth, then took a small swig from it, even though Williams protested.

"It tastes rather plummy," was Canning's verdict, as he strode over to the window and gazed out at the gathering twilight.

Saxon Hill mentioned that he and his sweetheart Leonora would be travelling to New York on the White Star liner *Adriatic* on the following day, producing an expensive diamond ring from his waistcoat pocket, he told Canning how he planned to propose to her on deck in the mid-Atlantic.

"You romantic fool, Saxon," laughed Canning, and the confectioner turned – to find Saxon Hill trembling all over his body. He seemed to be having some kind of fit. His eyes bulged alarmingly, and he wore an expression of sheer terror on his contorted face.

Williams noted Saxon's behaviour with a mixture of dread and curiosity.

"Saxon, what on earth's the matter, dear fellow?" asked Canning, going to the aid of his friend, but as he walked around the table he suddenly felt an intense, burning pain in the middle of his forehead, which forced his eyes to close tightly. Canning held his head in his hands and let out a horrible scream.

Saxon Hill was still standing, albeit with a rigid posture, despite the shuddering tremors which had gripped his body. He tried to utter something, but instead he began to foam at the mouth. His eyes seemed much whiter than normal and threatened to bulge out of their sockets. The foam frothed and dribbled down Hill's beard and on to his waistcoat.

Canning, meanwhile, was now face-down on the hearth rug, convulsing uncontrollably, and yelping the words, "Stop! Stop!"

At this point, a maidservant who had heard the commotion, barged into the drawing room and witnessed the horrendous sight of the two men gripped by some kind of strange insanity. As the servant looked on, Saxon Hill stumbled backwards into a corner and shielded his eyes with the back of his hand. With his bare hands, Thomas Canning started grabbing glowing pieces of coal from the fire and began hurling them at something only he could see on the floor.

Williams told the maid to fetch a doctor at once, and she closed the door and ran downstairs. She left the front door ajar and dashed across the road to the house of a Doctor Hamilton and informed him of the shocking scene she had just witnessed. When Hamilton and the maid entered the drawing room, they saw only Williams, initially, lying on the floor in obvious agony, clutching at his abdomen. Then the doctor and the maid heard the muffled sounds of someone crying. They traced the sobbing to Hill and Canning, who were cowering together under the table in abject terror.

Williams was taken to the Royal Infirmary on Pembroke Place, where an emergency appendectomy was carried out on him. He made a full recovery, and subsequently learned of the chilling fate of Saxon Hill and Thomas Canning who were not so lucky. Hill was being kept under lock and key in a room at the house of his brother, where he did nothing but tremble in a corner and mutter to himself. He had been certified insane and his family had been told that there was no hope of being cured. His sweetheart Leonora had sailed to America without him, and after learning of his insanity, had deserted him. Those who listened to Hill's ramblings said that he spoke of a hideous black squid, with a single green eye, that continuously coiled it's tentacles about him.

Thomas Canning's insanity made him a danger to himself as well as others, and he had been confined to a Lancashire lunatic asylum. He also told of being tormented by a repulsive tentacled creature that resembled a giant brown octopus, and of a long black panther, the size of a horse, which had glowing red eyes. Both creatures stalked him day and night. Canning felt so persecuted by the horrific creatures that he gouged out one of his own eyes in an attempt to blind himself. He later died in Bedlam lunatic asylum.

Saxon Hill never recovered and faded into obscurity.

Having destroyed the lives of two of his friends, not surprisingly, Williams abandoned his experiments with hallucinogens.

Drug researchers do not currently understand how Yage affects perception, and the noha grape used in the wine mixture is still banned in most countries.

THE GHOSTLY HARPIST

In the 1920s, the large Randall family of Kirkdale were forced to leave their crumbling home by the authorities, and they were moved to a large Victorian house on Everton Brow, which they found just as draughty and damp as their condemned home. It would be just a temporary move until more suitable accommodation could be found, they were told.

The Randalls soon settled into their temporary home, but it wasn't long before they realised that, as well as being uncomfortable, the place was haunted. It all started one stormy evening as the family gathered around the fire in the parlour, listening to their old Irish grandfather, Doogan. Doogan was telling the family one of his amusing tales of his youth in Dublin, when a strange, musical sound seemed to descend through the fabric of the house. At first everyone thought it was just the wind whistling down the chimney, as it was a stormy night, but when the gales quietened down, everyone could clearly distinguish what the sound was. Someone was playing a harp somewhere in one of the upstairs rooms.

One of the Randalls, a fifty-year-old navvy named Michael, came clattering down the uncarpeted stairs from his bedroom into the parlour. He'd been awakened from his slumbers by the eerie music, and had come to tell the rest of the family.

"We've heard it as well, Michael," said the Grandfather Doogan, and he added, "I don't like it at all. It's weird."

The grandaughters trembled and said, "What do you mean Grandad?"

Before he could answer, everyone jumped and the women shrieked as the corner of the table-cloth suddenly lifted. But it was only little Danny Randall, eleven years of age. He'd been listening to his grandfather's comments about the strange music, so he was now frightened as well. He emerged from under the table where he'd been playing, and clumsily stepped on his grandfather's shoe as he lunged towards him.

"Get over here, Danny," said Danny's mother through clenched teeth.

The grandfather uttered the dreaded word – "Ghosts."

Danny's father puffed hard on his pipe and his four sons listened to the ghostly melody. What was the song being played? thought the older people present. Although it was very faint, and difficult to hear because of the wind, they all found it familiar. Then Danny's grandmother identified the song. It was an old favourite called *Irish Rover*. The music gradually drifted away until only the sounds of the crackling fire filled the uneasy silence. No one dared to climb the stairs to go to bed until three in the morning.

At breakfast the next morning, a cousin of the Randalls called at the house. His name was Gerald Mooney. He spent his life travelling all over England to find work, and was nicknamed the Irish Rover by both friends and family. Strangely, no one connected his visit to the song *Irish Rover* played by the ghostly harp the night before.

Once it was daylight, the sons of the Randall family and their cousin Gerald Mooney felt a little more courageous. Together, they climbed up into the garret, right at the top of the house under the eaves. The door into the garret was swollen and warped with damp and could only be opened with great difficulty. The young men all pushed together and the door finally swung open, shaking loose a pile of dust that had probably been undisturbed for years. As their eyes adjusted to the darkness in the dusty attic, they each made out the unmistakable form of a large harp. It was about five feet in height and stood upright in the centre of the room, festooned with cobwebs and thick dust. Wiping away some of the cobwebs, the sons soon found the words 'Dublin 1872' inscribed on the body of the harp's metal frame. Realising that it must be valuable, they brushed it down and tried to play it but it sounded out of tune.

The young men stepped back on to the landing, choking from the dust. As the Randall sons were discussing what they should do with the harp and, more importantly, how much they would get for it and who they could sell it to, they heard the instrument playing all by itself. The young men slowly turned … a red-haired woman dressed in a long green dress was sitting at the harp, plucking the strings to produce a beautiful, lilting melody. Her face was too pale for her to be living, and her dark eyes glared at the five men with pure contempt, as if they were trespassing into her domain. The young men fell over one another as they ran pell-mell out of the garret.

No one in the family dared to go back up to the garret after that terrifying encounter with the phantom harpist, and on some nights, the family would hear her playing various melodies. These titles of these melodies always seemed to predict something. The sombre strains of *Molly Malone* were plucked by the phantasm in the garret one night, and by the following morning, Mrs Randall was visited by her brother – who brought her the sad news that their sister Molly had died in her sleep during the night. Was this a coincidence, or had the harpist's choice of melody been a warning of the death? On another occasion, the harpist played the *Mendelssohn's Wedding March*, and this was the very evening on which one of the Randall sons chose to come home to tell his family that his young lady had just accepted his proposal for marriage.

But one night the sound of a melody made everyone apprehensive. It was unmistakably *Danny Boy*, a song that had been based on a very old melody called *Londonderry Air*. There was a line in the song which went, 'It's you, it's you must go.' Did this mean that Danny, the youngest in the family, was going to go away, or worse still – going to die? The strange thing was that Danny Randall loved the song, and often asked his grandfather to sing it to him.

That week, Danny rode a friend's ricketty, homemade steering cart down the steep incline of Everton Brow, and he lost control of it and hit a brick wall, seriously injuring his head and his back. The boy was carefully carried into the house, and a doctor was sent for. By the time the doctor arrived, Danny was in a comatose state, and he said that, even if he was hospitalised, there was nothing that could be done to save him. Neurological know-how was very scant in those days and treatment for head injuries was very primitive, basically consisting of rest and quiet.

The family decided to keep Danny at home, where fervent Hail Marys were said for him and holy water was administered to his lips. The house which had always been filled with laughter and singing, was now filled with sadness. Everyone crept around on tiptoe and spoke in hushed whispers. And Danny hung on.

One stormy evening, as Danny's mother kept her vigil over her critically ill son, the family once again heard the ghostly strains of *Danny Boy* – the very same song that had seemed to foretell Danny's devastating accident. Suddenly, Danny's eyelids flickered, ever so slightly at first, then unmistakably – he was waking up! A miracle had happened! The next minute Danny opened his eyes fully as he finally woke up from his deathly coma. A faint smile was on his lips as he listened to his favourite song.

To the delight of his family, Danny went on to make a full recovery.

A month or so later, shortly before the Randalls left the haunted house for good, *Chopin's Death March* was clearly heard coming from the old harp in the garret, and each member of the family looked around at the others without saying a word. Each knew exactly what the others were thinking – Who will die tonight? They were right; that night, old Grandfather Doogan passed away at the house.

For years, there were strange rumours that the red-haired phantom harpist was the troubled spirit of a girl who had been murdered at the house in the eighteenth century.

THE HANGED MAN

One pleasant evening in June 1960, seven sixteen-year-olds sat, squashed together on a park bench, in Edge Hill's Botanic Gardens, either side of a Kensington lad named Tommy Murphy – or Spud Murphy as he was known to other members of the gang, because of his fondness for chips. They seemed to be hanging on to his every word.

Seventeen-year-old Spud was reading out an article from the *Liverpool Echo* about a local lad who had been caught trying to rob Wavertree's Abbey Cinema. Police had inspected the premises after a tip-off, but had found no one. They were about to leave, when the police dog, Rinty, started barking furiously at the empty seats of the auditorium. A sheepish boy soon emerged from behind one of the seats and gave himself up.

Spud's gang laughed at the idea of being caught by a dog. Spud said there was easy money to be made in the robbing of a factory. One of the boys, Billy, said that Edmundson's Sweets factory, off Wellington Road, was supposed to have a safe that was packed with money. Billy had overheard his uncle – who had once worked at the factory – talking about the safe. What's more, the safe's combination was kept on a piece of paper in a certain drawer of a filing cabinet in the same room. The factory's night-watchman was said to be a feeble old man. Even if the safe's contents couldn't be taken, Billy estimated that the sweet factory stock must be worth thousands – they could help themselves! The rest of the gang all said that they liked the idea and one of them suggested that they should all carry coshes, but Spud Murphy silenced them all when he claimed that he could get hold of a pistol. That would be the only weapon they'd need.

Later that week, Spud and his ten-year-old brother waited in an alleyway near Gerard Gardens until they saw their Uncle Alfie leaving for his local pub, as he did every night. They knew that he would be there for the next two hours – plenty of time to break into his flat and find what they were looking for. Spud levered open the bathroom window of the flat and then helped his brother to squeeze through the window to open the front door of the flat. Spud knew that Uncle Alfie kept an old loaded First World War Webley revolver hidden in his bedroom, in case he was burgled.

As Alfie was enjoying his nightly pints of ale at his local, Spud was rummaging through every drawer and cupboard in his bedroom until he found what he was looking for under the bed, beside a chamber pot. He examined the pistol's chambers and found that they were loaded with six bullets. Spud gave his little brother a ten shilling note for his part in the robbery and told him that he had better keep his mouth shut about what had happened that night. He then set off for his girlfriend's house with the pistol stuffed in his inside pocket.

His girlfriend, Susan, was horrified when Spud showed her the loaded pistol, and she cried her eyes out when Spud told her about the planned robbery.

"Don't be stupid, Spud," she cried. "You'll be hanged if you shoot anybody. It's not worth it. Throw that horrible thing away."

"No one's going to hang, and no one's going to get shot either!" Spud shouted at her.

At midnight, Spud and the seven members of his gang rendezvoused on Lawrence Road, then proceeded to the sweet factory on foot, in two groups of four. Most of the lads had never done anything worse than pinch a few penny sweets from the corner shop, and this was the first time any of them had been involved in anything as serious as this. They were all a bundle of nerves. Even Spud, for all his bravado, could feel his heart thumping in his chest, but he couldn't lose face now in front of the whole gang – they'd never listen to him again if he did.

As Spud and three others in his group were passing under the railway bridge that crosses Wellington Road, they came across a frightening sight. On the wall in front of them was projected the enormous shadow of someone hanging by the neck from a rope. They looked at each other, but said nothing. When the teenagers turned the corner they stopped in their tracks. A young man hung suspended from a girder of the railway bridge with a noose around his neck. His head was twisted at an unnatural angle and his eyes bulged in terror. His swollen, purple tongue protruded down past his chin, and from his throat came a hideous, bubbling, choking sound that chilled the would-be robbers to the bone.

Spud and the gang stood there under the swinging corpse, frozen in terror for a while, before fleeing in different directions. As Spud ran home, he told everybody he met about the hanged man. One or more of them must have dialled 999, because a police car and an ambulance rushed to the railway bridge within minutes. No hanged man, or any evidence of a hanging, such as a rope with a noose, was found anywhere near the scene.

The ill-fated robbery was abandoned, and the next day Spud surreptitiously returned the revolver to his uncle's flat and he even helped him put his things back together, although he did not admit to him that he and his brother had actually perpetrated the break-in. From that day onwards, Spud went straight, as he believed that the vision of the hanged man had been some sort of supernatural omen, warning him that he would face the hangman if he shot anybody during the robbery. The rest of the gang all breathed a sigh of relief.

THE CASE OF THE UNBORN DAUGHTER

In 1999, thirty-two-year-old Patrick from Aigburth, experienced a series of paranormal experiences that left him a changed man. They all began one Friday in the October of that year.

Patrick was unemployed and single, and he was leading a pretty aimless, depressing existence. On Fridays he usually dragged himself out of bed at around eleven in the morning, before setting off to cash his Girocheque at the Post Office. After collecting his money, he would call round to his friend Steve's house, and the two of them would then drive around aimlessly in Steve's car, without any particular purpose or destination in mind. They would just cruise around the neighbourhood, with Steve beeping the horn of his car at any women they found attractive. And Fridays were the highlight of Patrick's week!

On this particular Friday, Patrick and Steve went to the local pub, and proceeded to get thoroughly drunk on Patrick's Giro money. Several hours later they staggered to the local take-away to get themselves a kebab and some chips. On the way, they attempted to chat up two girls, who, like many others before them, rejected their drunken advances and stormed off in a huff. Steve then caught a taxi home, and Patrick walked unsteadily back to his flat, weaving drunkenly from one side of the pavement to the other. After finally managing to get his key into the keyhole in the front door, he let himself in.

Once inside, he flopped down on the sofa, which was littered with crumbs, newspapers and half-eaten chocolate bars, and drunkenly began to contemplate his lonely, futile existence. His mood sank lower and lower, and he decided to switch on the television to try and rid his mind of his depressing thoughts. He was still so intoxicated that he couldn't figure out how to change channels and he sat there, befuddled, watching an Open University programme on BBC2 until two in the morning.

Just as he was thinking about going to bed, a little girl, aged about five or six, came skipping into the living room. She was wearing pretty pink pyjamas covered with teddy bears, and she had long, glossy, black hair which was gleaming as though it had just been washed. She jumped on to the sofa and threw her arms around Patrick's neck, then snuggled her loveable round face into his chest. Patrick was in a state of shock. Still suffering from the effects of all the alcohol he had drunk, he initially thought his sister Sandra had somehow got into the flat with her little daughter Kerry. But this child was nothing like Kerry, by any stretch of the imagination.

"Who are you?" Patrick finally managed to stammer.

The little face looked up into his astonished face, her beautiful large green eyes staring right into his.

"I'm your daughter, Daddy," she said, with a serious expression on her face, "but I haven't been born yet."

As Patrick tried to digest the strange reply, the girl vanished before his eyes, yet for a while he could still feel the child's weight on his lap and chest, and smell her fragrant, newly-washed hair.

Patrick stood up, suddenly feeling stone-cold sober, and wondered if his friend Steve had spiked his drink with some narcotic substance. He went to bed, and twice during the night, he distinctly felt the phantom child hugging him. He was more fascinated than afraid.

Over the next few nights he had very vivid dreams that he was with the little girl, and in one dream, the child begged, "Daddy, please find my mummy, or I'll never be born! Please, Daddy!" Then the child started to cry her eyes out. Patrick promised her that he would do as she asked, and he woke with hot tears stinging his eyes.

What was happening to him? Was he losing his mind? Who was the sweet little child who kept on calling her Daddy?

Patrick decided to tell Steve about his strange experiences, as he was the only friend he had to confide in. However, Steve was not the fanciful type – he didn't believe in dreams and the supernatural – and Patrick's attempt to pour his heart out, went straight over his sceptical friend's head.

"What you need is a session down the pub," was Steve's unhelpful response.

"No, I'm sick of all that," said Patrick, angrily. "What's the point?"

Steve stopped smiling, "Okay, you're on your own then," he snapped. "You're losing it, mate."

For months Patrick had been saying that he was going to go back to college, but for some reason he hadn't been able to motivate himself to actually go and do it. Somehow, his strange encounter with the little girl had given him the impetus he needed. The following day he got up early and set off for the local further education college, where he enrolled on a computer course. He quickly found that he had an aptitude for computers and was soon doing so well that it was clear he would be able to find a career in IT. Whilst he was there, he was introduced to a pretty young student called Paula, and he ended up dating her. The relationship quickly became serious, Patrick had never met anyone like her before. They married in July 2000.

In May 2001, Patrick, who was now in full-time employment, became the proud father of a little girl whom he and his wife decided to call Amy. She was born with a full head of glossy, black hair. His wife and baby daughter have transformed his life, and he is absolutely sure that the spirit of his unborn daughter somehow crossed over into the aimless, layabout world in which he was living, to help her future father change the direction of his life.

STILL DOING HIS ROUNDS

Wartime, like any other, throws up supernatural mysteries which are difficult to explain away in ordinary terms. Here are two strange tales relating to the Second World War.

I mentioned the following ghostly after-image of the Second World War in the first volume of *Haunted Liverpool*, and as a result I have received a steady stream of letters and emails over the years from people who have actually seen the ghost, and also from those who have learned about the apparition through their parents, or grandparents.

~

Thirty years after the May Blitz, in August 1971, a ghostly vestige of World

War Two put in an appearance on Scotland Road in broad daylight. People living near Lawrence Gardens were intrigued by the sight of an odd-looking man dressed in an old police uniform. He wore an anti-shrapnel helmet and had a khaki haversack slung over his shoulder. Many witnesses saw him as he walked along, tapping on doors, windows and a lamppost with his truncheon. One curious woman decided to follow him but, upon turning a corner, she saw nothing. The World War Two policeman had simply vanished into thin air.

There were many more sightings of the ghostly bobby, and some older folk in the area actually recognised him. He was the local beat officer who had died in a bombing raid on Scotland Road during the May Blitz. In order to warn illegal gamblers that he was about – and to also assure the law-abiding citizens that he was on his rounds – the constable had developed the habit of tapping on windows and doors with his truncheon as he walked his beat.

After he had been killed, local people missed the reassuring rattle of his truncheon as he walked his round. They liked to feel that someone was watching over them. Perhaps he came back from the grave because he was aware of this, and wanted to put their minds at rest.

EVERY CLOUD ...

This short black humorous tale also dates from the war years. Twelve-year-old Tony from the West Derby area of Liverpool, desperately wanted a bicycle for his birthday, and despite his father's protestations – a child's bicycle was a real luxury in those days – his mother purchased the bike from Lewis's department store 'on the tick'.

Each night the boy's father would argue that the family could hardly make ends meet as it was, let alone make weekly payments for a useless bike. None of the other children in the street owned a bike and he didn't see why Tony should be any different. The arguments between Tony's warring parents often became so heated that, on more than one occasion, they actually came to blows. To make matters worse, Tony's bike sustained an irreparable puncture just days after he was given it on his birthday.

Tony got down on his knees beside his bed one night and fervently prayed for God to somehow make the people in Lewis's forget about the payments which were still owed on the accursed bike. He wished he'd never asked for it in the first place.

On the following evening, Lewis's store was completely destroyed by the Luftwaffe's bombs during the May Blitz, and all the hire-purchase records were incinerated as a result. All records of the debt owed for the bike were wiped away – courtesy of a German bomb!

Every cloud certainly does have a silver lining!

THE LAST TIME I SAW CLANCY

Over the years, many people have asked me if there was any truth in the story about the dog that swam across the River Mersey in the 1950s. Well, I asked the public for information about this incident numerous times when I was on the radio, and from the accounts related to me as a result, I have pieced together the following strange tale.

In the early 1950s, thirteen-year-old Paul was strolling past one of the farms that used to exist off Childwall Valley Road, when he noticed a hand-written sign hanging on the fence which said: 'Labrador Puppies For Sale. Enquire within'. Paul had always longed for a dog of his own, and when he saw Farmer Jackson rolling a milk churn down the lane, he eagerly ran up to him and asked him how much he was selling the pups for.

"Six shillings each," said Jackson, gruffly, as he hoisted the heavy churn up on to the stone platform outside the farm gate. As he was shutting the five-bar gate, a sleek black Labrador emerged from the kennel, with six tiny pups stumbling after her. A seventh pup followed them out of the kennel and seemed to have trouble walking. It was very skinny and weak-looking and was half the size of the other six.

"I've only got two shillings, Mr Jackson," said Paul, pulling a handful of coppers out of the pocket of his shorts and laboriously counting it in his palm.

In a cold voice, the farmer said: "Well, you'll need another four, son. These are all pure Labradors."

Paul turned disconsolately away from the gate, when the farmer called him back and grudgingly said, "Go on then, give me what you've got, and take him." Jackson pointed to the seventh pup, the skinny one that was staggering around the yard on its wobbly little legs.

Paul was reluctant at first, and asked the farmer why the pup had such difficulty walking. The farmer scooped up the puppy and handed him to Paul.

"He was the last born of the litter, the runt, that's why he's so small," said Jackson. "Make your mind up. Do you want him or not? I haven't got all day."

As soon as Paul held the tiny furry bundle in his hand he was smitten, and he handed Jackson the two shillings. Farmer Jackson tutted at the handful of ha'pennies and pennies, but Paul didn't even notice. He stroked the tiny puppy, which looked at him with its big round eyes and licked his fingers.

On his way home, Paul met a girl named Clancy Jones – a girl he had a teenage crush on. Clancy made a huge fuss of the pup and stroked it and squeezed it in her arms. To impress her, Paul said that he would be naming the pup Clancy. Clancy was very touched by the gesture and gave Paul a quick peck on the cheek. Paul blushed bright red, and his heart fluttered as he watched Clancy walk on down the lane.

When the boy returned home with Clancy the pup, his widowed mother was furious. She said she could just about afford to keep herself and Paul, never mind a sickly dog. Paul was crestfallen, but at least his mother had said that he would be allowed to keep the pup for a few weeks until she found someone she could give it to.

A week later, Paul's spinster aunt in Waterloo died unexpectedly, and in her will, she left her house off Crosby Road to Paul's mother, and this house had a garden back and front. Barely able to believe their good fortune, Paul and his mother moved into the house, along with the pup Clancy. The dog soon grew stronger and started to walk properly, and Paul used to take it to the local playing fields each day for a long runaround.

Paul and Clancy became inseparable, and Paul soon realised that the animal had more senses than the average dog. Clancy had amazing hearing, and it also seemed as if he could tell the time, because each evening he would look at the dial of the clock when it was 5.30pm, and would run to the hallway, waiting for Paul's mother to come home.

In 1952, Paul had been fantasising that he was a prospector in a log cabin in Alaska in the hut at the bottom of the garden. He fell asleep in the hut reading a comic by candlelight. Anyway, the candle burnt down to its base and the hot wax soaked into the wooden tabletop and ignited.

Meanwhile, Paul's mother was in the kitchen, making the tea, when she saw something amazing. The hose-pipe had been left unwound in the back garden, but left attached to the standpipe. Clancy had the end of the hosepipe in his mouth, and he had it trained on the hut, which was billowing with smoke. Paul's mother rushed out and had to force the door open. Paul was dragged out coughing and spluttering, and when his mum was sure that he was okay, she scolded him for lighting candles in the hut. Then they hugged each other, realising what a close escape he had had.

However, Paul and his mum were baffled as to who had turned the tap on to feed the hose-pipe – surely Clancy wasn't that clever – but they soon discovered that he was. In the summer, they watched him craftily tilt his head and grab the tap with his teeth and turn it on. He would then seize the end of the hosepipe and playfully spray the water about, aiming it especially at the cat next door. Clancy was very crafty and only did this when he thought no one was watching.

On another occasion he went missing, and Paul and his mother found him sitting on a neighbour's doorstep, staring solemnly at the door. The old woman who lived there often gave Clancy fish scraps on a Friday, but this was a Sunday. The dog began to howl at the door. Paul and his mum had never heard Clancy make such an weird, mournful sound. Later that day, the old woman's daughter entered the house and found her mother lying dead in bed. She looked very peaceful and had a slight smile on her face. It turned out that her mother had died in bed that morning, but how did Clancy know that?

In the summer of 1953, on Paul's birthday, he went to the Pier Head, ready to embark on a voyage to New Brighton with his cousin and a friend. With him, on a leash, was Clancy, carrying a plastic bucket in his mouth. Long before the ferry arrived, a gang of bullies confronted Paul and one of them snatched a bag of sweets from him. Clancy sensed that the gang's intentions were to harm Paul, and he growled at them. The biggest member of the gang put the sole of his foot on the dog's back and cruelly pushed him through the safety railings. Paul held on to Clancy's leash, but his collar slipped off. The tide was in and the waters of the Mersey were high, and the dog yelped as it tumbled into the muddy, swirling waters. The strong currents soon carried the dog out into the Mersey, and Paul watched him helplessly and began to cry.

A group of adults chased off the gang of bullies, then they tried to comfort Paul. He pushed away from them and watched Clancy's head bobbing up and down in the choppy water. It looked as if the dog was trying to swim against the current towards the opposite shore, in an effort to stop himself from being washed out to sea. Paul and his cousin boarded the ferry to Birkenhead, hoping that the dog would make it to the other side of the river.

When they reached Birkenhead, they checked the waterfront, and a woman told them that a dog had crawled up the moss-coated stone steps from the water to the promenade about twenty minutes before. She had tried to go to the animal's aid but it seemed very frightened and ran off. Paul and his cousin scoured the area, but could find no trace of Clancy.

Then Paul came upon a terrible sight; staring out of the back of a dog-catcher's van, was the unmistakable face of Clancy, still wet and bedraggled from his ordeal in the river. Paul and his cousin dashed after the van but it drove off before they could reach it.

Paul's mother didn't have a telephone, and the boy never thought about going to the police. He and his cousin caught the ferry back to Liverpool, then boarded a tram home, where they told his mother about the bullies and Clancy's ordeal. The next day she visited the local dogs' home and the RSPCA and made enquiries about a black Labrador, but she was told that there were no dogs of that description in the kennels. Paul was so distraught, that he and his mother ended up travelling back to Birkenhead to search for Clancy. When they finally located the kennels where he had been taken, the dog catcher sadly shook his head and said, "I'm sorry, love. I'm afraid the Labrador was put to sleep. He was in such a bad state. Been in the river by the looks of things."

Paul and his mother returned to Liverpool with heavy hearts, knowing that they would never find another dog like Clancy.

Paul is now in his sixties, and he tells how, about a year after Clancy died, he was awakened at about four in the morning, by something licking his hand. When he gazed into the darkness, he could just about make out the familiar face of Clancy. He is positive that what he experienced wasn't a dream, or any kind of hallucination; the dog was there – he could feel him and smell him. The face of his devoted canine friend then melted away slowly into the darkness.

GHOSTLY BYSTANDERS

In 1997, thirty-five-year-old Greg from Bootle left his girlfriend's flat on Sheil Road just after three o'clock in the morning. He put on his safety helmet and mounted his 250cc Honda Super Dream motorcycle and drove off into the freezing cold night. Greg travelled up Belmont Road, turned right into Breck Road, and then, seeing that Priory Road looked deserted, he gave his motorbike full throttle and accelerated as he performed a wheelie, with the front wheel of the bike in the air. As Greg tore past Stanley Park, his bike seemed to hit what felt like a stretch of black ice, and he lost control of the machine, then hit a brick wall. It all happened so fast, it seemed unreal.

Greg woke up surrounded by a crowd of bystanders. He immediately realised that his left arm was paralysed, and assumed that it was broken. Both of his legs felt completely numb. He groaned and one of the bystanders – an old man with a white moustache and a flat cap – leaned over Greg and said, "Hold on there, son. Help will come soon."

Greg looked to his left and saw a woman of about fifty years of age looking down at him. She wore a long black dress that went down to her ankles. She was smiling at Greg, and she suddenly whispered something that annoyed and terrified him at the same time.

"He's a goner," she said, to no one in particular. "The shock'll kill him."

A few other members of the crowd that Greg couldn't see muttered in agreement with the morbid woman.

Greg reached inside his leather jacket with his uninjured hand and frantically felt for his mobile phone. His hand shook as he retrieved the phone, and he held it out to the old man and said, "Phone for an ambulance. Quick."

The old man recoiled from the telephone as if it was a gun. He gazed at it with a puzzled look and said nothing in reply.

Greg couldn't understand why the old man refused to take the phone from him. He offered it to another man standing over him, but he too just stood there without accepting the mobile. Then something happened which threw a supernatural light on to the proceedings.

There came a sudden gust of wind which disturbed the flowing, ankle-length skirt of the woman who had predicted that Greg wouldn't survive the crash. There were no feet or shoes at the end of that skirt when it fluttered in the wind – just empty space. Only then did Greg realise that the people surrounding him were not people at all, but ghosts. Twenty feet away from where he lay was the wall of Anfield Cemetery. When Greg gazed up once more at the face of the woman, she was gazing down at him with a grinning expression that made his flesh creep.

A hackney cab suddenly screeched to a halt at the scene and the taxi driver jumped out and knelt beside Greg to reassure him that he'd just called for an ambulance. Greg pointed to the figures, which were now slowly dispersing, but the cabby obviously couldn't see the ghostly bystanders. Greg watched as each of the figures left the scene of the crash and walked, one by one, back through the wall of Anfield Cemetery.

Within the space of a few minutes, an ambulance had arrived and, after treating Greg at the scene, they took him away to hospital. He survived the crash, despite his very serious injuries. He told the staff at the hospital about the ghosts who had surrounded him after the motorbike smash. One of the nurses revealed that many years before a similar incident had taken place at the same spot. A motorist who had crashed on Walton Lane was brought into casualty, and he swore that the crowd of bystanders who had come upon the scene before the ambulance had slowly melted away as the paramedics arrived.

DEATHS FORETOLD

On Saturday, 8 March 2003, at 2am, the actor and former pop star Adam Faith died from a heart attack. He was sixty-two. Faith had been staying at a hotel in Stoke-on-Trent, Staffordshire, where he was starring in the Regent Theatre's *Love and Marriage*. He was rushed to hospital, but doctors fought in vain to resuscitate the actor who had a history of heart trouble.

As the showbiz world mourned the loss of the Sixties entertainer, who had also starred in the popular *Budgie* television series, BBC Radio Merseyside's Alec Young recalled an eerie phone call from a listener who had telephoned the radio station on the previous Thursday, 6 March. A man who only identified himself as "Ken of Southport" telephoned the station, and Alec Young took the call. Ken told Alec that the singer Adam Faith had just died.

Alec mentioned this to other members of the station's staff, but the claim couldn't be broadcast until it could be confirmed by the radio station's newsroom. The radio journalists had most definitely not received any information of any kind to verify Adam Faith's death. Alec Young checked the newspapers and Ceefax, but there was not one iota of news about Adam Faith – so Alec decided that it would not be wise to comment about Ken's mysterious call on air.

When Adam Faith's death was announced on the following Saturday, Alec's jaw dropped.

"It was like something out of the *Twilight Zone*. I thought about the call I'd received at the radio station on the previous Thursday from Ken of Southport," Alec told me.

Alec Young mentioned this strange incident to listeners on Monday afternoon, and he urged Ken of Southport to get back in touch. As of yet, Ken has not contacted the radio station …

~

This incident reminded me of another death in the show business world that was allegedly foretold in a supernatural manner. Film star Vincent Price was a good friend of another Hollywood star, the handsome heart-throb, Tyrone Power.

One afternoon in November 1958, Price was flying into New York airport when the weather was particularly bad, so the plane had to circle the heavy grey clouds which were hanging over the Big Apple. Price was reading a book, when suddenly he felt a strange and powerful urge to push aside the curtain from his window. He peered through the porthole window at the grey and dismal sky, and then the actor's heart palpitated wildly when he saw something in the clouds that would haunt him for the rest of his life.

In glowing crimson letters across the lowering New York sky, the chilling message, 'TYRONE POWER IS DEAD' was spelt out.

Vincent Price couldn't believe what he was seeing. He turned to a woman sleeping in the next seat and shook her awake, then pointed out of the window to draw her attention to the bizarre message etched across the oppressive sky, but the woman could see nothing of the sort, because the illuminated message was no longer there.

As soon as the plane had landed, Price rushed down the steps of the aircraft and asked several members of the airport police if they had seen the sentence flashed up on the clouds, but the police, who didn't recognise him, shook their heads and just smirked – another nutter!

Price then walked over to a news stand and scanned the headlines of the *New York Times*; there was no mention of Tyrone Power's death. When Price checked into a hotel, a theatrical agent he'd worked with many years before approached him in the foyer and grabbed his arm, saying, "Vincent, have you heard the terrible news? Tyrone Power died of a heart attack half an hour ago. You were good friends, weren't you?"

So it was true, Tyrone was dead. Price felt an icy cold tingle go down his spine like an electric shock; half an hour ago he had seen the strange aerial obituary in glowing letters in the grey, New York sky. How had it happened? What strange forces were at work that he did not understand?

Up to the time of his death, Vincent Price was haunted by the memory of the eerie message emblazoned on the clouds on that dismal rainy afternoon.

THE MAN IN BLACK

One evening in 1932, on the night of a full moon, nine people arrived at a house in St John's Road in Waterloo. Some of the nosier neighbours, twitching their net curtains, wondered what the nature of the gathering was. Was some party imminent perhaps? Was it somebody's birthday? Had they known the truth, they would have been scandalised, for the people were actually assembling for a séance. It is an ancient belief that the number of people attending a séance should be divisible by three, and so these nine people from Waterloo, Crosby and Litherland seated themselves around a large round table in an upstairs room, ready for what some of them regarded as a bit of fun, and others as an adventure into the unknown.

In the centre of the table was a loaf of bread. Bread placed in the middle of the table in such a way is also part of an age-old custom, and is thought to attract the spirits for some obscure reason. Three candles were lit around the bread, and the heavy velvet curtains were drawn and overlapped so that not even a single ray of moonlight could enter the room. The men and women each spread their hands out on the table so that they touched one another by the tips of their little fingers. The participants then intoned these words together:

"Spirit, we bring you gifts from life into death. Commune with us, spirit, and move among us."

Everyone present waited eagerly for a response.

Two raps from the spirit were expected, and the sitters waited in tense silence. This was the first time a séance had been held at this particular address on St John's Road. Other séances held by the group at other addresses had all been huge anti-climaxes. Little did anyone know that this address held a terrible dark secret. This was one house where supernatural dabblings of any kind should definitely not have been carried out.

The sound of a clock striking midnight could be heard in the living room downstairs. The candles started to flicker on the table, and as the midnight chimes started to fade, everyone felt something vibrating through the table. The floor and the entire room began to shake. Then, suddenly, the curtains flew fully open as if pulled apart by invisible hands – to reveal a sinister figure in a long black cape standing there. The strange outdated figure was seen as a silhouette because of the full moon shining down behind it through the window. It flitted forward towards the startled people at the table, and it placed its hand on the shoulder of the man acting as the medium of the table. This man shuddered because, even through his clothes, he could feel that the hand of the supernatural stranger was colder than ice. Everybody then gasped in fear and amazement as the figure vanished instantly with a loud flutter of its cape.

The gas lamps on the wall were quickly lit, and everybody wondered what the significance of the sinister vision was, and why it had touched the medium's shoulder. Everybody agreed that the man in the black cloak had given off a strong aura of evil which had permeated the whole room.

On the following morning, the medium from that séance – who lived in Crosby – was found dead in his bed, and on his pallid face, was a look of the utmost horror.

The case then deepened when other members of the séance discovered from various people in St John's Road that the place where they had held the séance had quite a reputation for being haunted. The man in black with the long cloak had put in an appearance at least forty years before, and he was reputed to be a harbinger of death.

Now, I was intrigued to receive a letter in early 2003 from a Mrs Stephenson who once lived at the haunted house in Waterloo, but who now lives in Australia. She said that, in 1976, a female relative was returning home one night, just after nine o'clock, and as she entered the house, which was in total darkness, she noticed a faint glow at the top of the stairs, and silhouetted against this glow was the figure of a man in a cape. The woman froze in fear, and cried out, "Who's that?" When there was no reply, she realised that she was seeing the spectre she had often heard her mother talk about. It was supposed to appear when one of the family was about to come to harm. On previous occasions it had put in an appearance before the death of her grandmother, and on another occasion it had materialised days before her brother had suffered a heart attack.

The woman panicked because she was convinced that the phantom was going to attack her. It definitely gave out a strong impression of menace. When the woman switched the light on, the figure instantly disappeared.

Nine days later, the woman's brother was seriously injured in a car crash, but fortunately recovered. The figure was about 5ft 10in in height, had short black hair, and wore a cloak that covered its legs.

In 1987, Mrs Stephenson emigrated to Australia with her family and young daughter. Then, a few years ago, she returned to Waterloo, and during the visit, she and her brother and daughter went to visit the old house on St John's Road to reminisce, and during the visit her daughter disappeared. She had wandered off by herself into a room upstairs. This girl had never been told about the incidents with the man in black. When her mother caught up with her, she was trembling. Something had obviously upset her. She told her mother that a man's voice had urged her to pick up a piece of glass which was lying on the floor from a broken window, and to use it to slash her wrists. He had then added: "It won't hurt; you will only feel cold for a short while."

Mrs Stevenson had heard enough. She grabbed hold of her daughter's hand and pulled her out of the accursed house.

The identity of the man in black remains a mystery.

CORA VERSUS THE GHOSTS

In December 1975, thirteen-year-old Cora and her forty-five-year-old mother Jackie, moved into a house in the Islington area of Liverpool. Cora's father had died three years previously from a heart condition, and her mother still hadn't really got over her loss, or found anyone who could take his place.

At Christmas, Cora received a lot of gifts from her mother, aunts and grandmother, and among these was the distant ancestor of the Play Station – a primitive electronic video game called 'Pong'. The game was an electronic version of ping-pong played on a domestic television screen. The ball was nothing more than a square blip that bounced back and forth across the television screen between two on-screen paddles that could only move up and down when the players turned two corresponding dials. The ball made a loud bleeping sound when it bounced off the paddles. A child today would quickly tire of such a rudimentary video game, but in 1975, children – and adults – happily played Pong for hours.

One evening Cora and her friend Sally were playing Pong as they chatted about boys, clothes, pop songs, and similar topics that teenaged girls often talk about. Sally's mother called at the house at 9.30pm to say that it was time for her daughter to go home. Sally left, and when Cora went back into the living room, she was surprised to hear the bleeping sounds still coming from the Pong video game console. The paddles on the screen were moving up and down, and the ball was ricocheting between them. Something was playing with the video game.

"Mum!" shouted Cora, and she turned and ran into the kitchen where her mother was doing the washing up. Cora excitedly told her about the strange incident taking place in the living room and urged her to come and have a look for herself. Grabbing a tea towel and wiping the suds from her hands, Jackie followed her daughter into the living room. The white luminous blip of the ball beeped as it bounced randomly across the screen. The paddles were stationary now. The ghost, or whatever it was, had ceased playing with the game.

"Something was playing the game, Mum. I swear!" Cora said, with obvious sincerity.

Jackie had never known her daughter to lie, and felt uneasy as she listened to Cora's spooky account.

Cora and her mother retired to their beds at 11pm, but at three in the morning they were awakened by a low rumbling sound that seemed to shake the whole house to its foundations. Jackie leapt from her bed and ran downstairs, thinking there had been a gas explosion or an earth tremor, but downstairs everything seemed fine. Jackie could find nothing to explain the earth-shaking phenomenon. As Jackie left the living room, she bumped into Cora, who had also crept downstairs to investigate the origin of the tremor. Jackie yelped with fright and Cora giggled and apologised.

Cora returned to her bed, and her mother went back to her own bedroom. Cora had only been asleep for a few minutes when suddenly she woke up and saw, to her horror, that the walls of her room were moving inwards, closing in on her. She tried to rationalise what she was seeing, she knew that logically it was impossible, yet the room was definitely getting smaller. Not only that, but the teenager found that her whole body was paralysed, and she began to suffer a sensation of being suffocated.

As she struggled to breathe, a putrid, stomach-turning odour filled her nostrils, making her want to retch. Cora had the sensation of something pressing down on her, and in her mind she caught glimpses of bodies lying about in heaps. Many of these bodies were actually lying on top of her. The room grew darker, and suddenly, the voice of a young boy screamed out: "Connie!"

Cora started to pray. She fervently muttered the Lord's Prayer, and almost instantly, the walls of her bedroom reverted to normality, and the unpleasant heavy sensation of pressure on her body vanished, along with the hideous, filthy smell. Cora sat bolt upright in bed, gasping for breath, then quickly got up and turned on the light.

Several days later, Cora's friend Sally was sitting in the front parlour of the house, browsing through a magazine, when she suddenly had the eerie feeling that she was being watched. She cautiously looked over the top of the magazine and there were three figures: a boy, aged about ten, a girl of about sixteen, and an old man. They were all dressed in old-fashioned clothes. Their faces looked very pale and sickly, and their eyes were dark and sunken. Sally let out a strangled scream and the figures vanished.

Cora came running into the parlour and instantly noticed the same rank smell that had manifested itself in her bedroom during the terrifying episode that had occurred a few nights before. Sally refused to stay in the parlour and quickly left the house after telling Cora what she had seen. Cora's mother Jackie saw the ghosts of a young boy and a teenaged girl days later, standing on the stairs, mournfully gazing at her with those creepy dark eyes. The figures slowly vanished as Jackie looked on in shock. Jackie suggested to her daughter that perhaps they should leave the property as it was obviously haunted, but Cora was a very brave and determined girl, and she said that she wasn't going to be defeated by a bunch of ghosts; she was going to fight them.

Cora set off for the Central Library and read everything she could find about exorcism. She scooped holy water into a bottle from the font in the local church, and borrowed a large, wall-mounted crucifix and a family Bible from the home of her grandmother, who was a devout Roman Catholic. An ornamental bell which she found in the house would also be of great use in the rite of bell book and candle, which she had read about in the library. Jackie urged her daughter not to dabble with supernatural matters and still thought they should leave the house, but the child was adamant about confronting the ghosts. They were preventing her from sleeping, they had scared her best friend out of the house, and they simply did not belong there.

Jackie put her hands to her face and sat trembling in the living room as Cora performed the exorcism. She splashed holy water about as she quoted from the Psalms and passages of the Bible. Many candles were lit, and Cora held the crucifix out at the places where the ghosts had appeared. Closely following the instructions in the library book, she said aloud: "I abjure thee and summon thee to leave this place in the name of Jesus Christ!"

Weird groaning sounds started to fill the house, and a musky smell circulated on a draught which came from nowhere. Jackie called up the stairs and pleaded with her daughter to stop the exorcism rite. She shouldn't be dabbling with forces she didn't understand. But young Cora took no notice. The bell was rung, which seemed to stir up the sinister breeze and it attacked the candles, making their flames splutter.

After the longest hour in Jackie's life, her daughter, looking pale and drawn, finally came back downstairs and announced, "It's okay, Mum. They've gone and they won't be back."

Cora was right. The ghosts never did return. Perhaps it was just imagination or autosuggestion, but on the following day, when the sun shone, the rooms in the house all seemed brighter, and a fresh, sweet aroma unaccountably permeated the air. Sally was eventually persuaded to return to the house, and her friendship with Cora continued to blossom. Today, Sally and Cora are still the best of friends.

What supernatural forces had been haunting the house?

Well, an old woman named Maggie told Cora's mother that the house had had a reputation for being haunted for some time. Maggie's mother had told her that the area of Liverpool where the haunted house stood had once been consumed by a terrible plague of cholera. In that quarter of the town, the dead were brought out and thrown on to a cart piled high with decaying bodies. Groans were sometimes heard to come from some of the bodies, so the cholera victims obviously weren't always dead when they were taken away to the secret burial pits.

Apparently, a grandfather, his granddaughter and grandson, who had lived at the infamous house of spirits, had succumbed to the plague, and their bodies were unceremoniously thrown on to a cart, atop the tangled knot of other corpses. Not long afterwards, it was said that the phantoms of the grandfather, granddaughter and grandson were seen and heard at the empty house. Over the years, the visitations had become less frequent and intense. So what had provoked the sudden recurrence of the hauntings was not known, and Cora was never able to find out.

However, Cora researched the story which Liz had told her, and discovered that in 1849 Asiatic cholera visited Liverpool. In a crumbling old book, she uncovered this eyewitness account of the epidemic:

People were dying all around me in dozens; neighbours might be talking at their front doors at dusk with each other, and by morning most would be dead. Every morning a cart would come round, preceded by a man with a red flag, who cried, "Bring out your dead". No coffin was there, not even a shroud, as the corpses were lifted out of the cellars and kitchens. Anywhere they fell stricken, and were thrown on to the cart. Two or three might be taken from one house, and on several occasions I heard moans from the bodies as they lay in the cart, showing they were not dead. They were all carried out to Bootle to be interred without shrouds or coffins in a common grave.

Cora researched the cholera plague incident further, and discovered that in 1849, the year of the outbreak, sixty-nine-year-old George Green had lived at her house, along with his granddaughter Connie, aged fifteen, and her brother Alfred, aged nine. Cora cast her mind back to that night when she had felt the walls closing in on her and the sensation of being squashed under a pile of

79

bodies. She had distinctly heard the sound of a boy crying out the name Connie.

Cora and her mother moved from their home in the 1980s, and today the house no longer stands.

RESIDENTIAL GHOST

To earn some money during the summer school holidays, seventeen-year-old Penny from Wirral, took a job at a local residential home for the elderly. Situated at the end of her road, the attractive building had always intrigued her, standing, towering and stately, on the corner of the meandering pathway through to the park. She passed it every day on her way to and from school, and had always wondered what it must have been before it became a residential home.

On the first day she started work as a temporary care assistant, she was extremely nervous, cautiously making her way up the gravel path towards the brass knocker on the intimidating red, double-fronted main door. After an echoing knock that seemed to shake the very foundations of the place, she heard heavy footsteps approaching the door, which was then opened and she was greeted by a stern but friendly matron.

On that first day she noticed that the framed photographs lining the walls in the entrance hall showed that the building had been used as a hospital during and after the First World War, but she couldn't quell her romanticised imaginings of the fabulous building having once been some aristocrat's abode, bustling with society's élite, with the kitchens and ground floor hectic with busy servants.

She settled into the job with no problems, and enjoyed helping the elderly residents. Often, she would even go in and visit them on her lunch break. Many of them were real characters, with interesting stories of the past to share with any young and eager ears willing to listen. Quite a number of them were bed-ridden for one reason or another and glad of the company, if anyone could find the time to pop in with their afternoon cup of tea and join them for a few minutes. It was during one of these particular visits that Penny first learned the history of the building and its original owners.

It was an old lady called Muriel who had lived in the area since childhood, who remembered the tale which her mother had told her about the wealthy landowner who had lived in the building in the early 1900s. Indeed, it had been a grand house belonging to a widower who lived there with his only daughter, Emily. A lively young girl, with bright blonde ringlets and a prettily dimpled chin, she had the run of the huge premises, including the vast and blooming garden where she particularly loved to dance and play.

Muriel's voice softened as she explained that years later, in the 1950s, the house had been renovated, and where the kitchen extension now stood, there had once been a raised well, where Emily, despite her father's repeated warnings about the dangers of playing near the well, had made many a wish and thrown many a coin in hope and expectation. That well was also where Emily fell one summer afternoon, as her father busily tackled a bundle of mail in his study. Apparently, nobody heard her scream as she stumbled to her doom. The servants chatting in the basement as they loaded the pantry with the recently-delivered fresh meat, the maids in the parlour polishing the silver before dinner, the cook in the kitchen preparing a rich stock for the last meal of the day, were all too busy to hear Emily's fading cries.

Emily's petite body lay slumped and lifeless at the bottom of the deep well for many hours while her mystified father searched for her late into the night.

Muriel explained to Penny in hushed tones that the poor father had been devastated by his second terrible loss. It was said that the ghost of little Emily still haunted the long corridors and hallways of the old house, searching for a friend to play with.

Muriel's tale sent a shiver down Penny's spine. She glanced at her watch and realised that her shift had started again some minutes ago, so she rushed back to work and the haunting story was pushed to the back of her mind.

That was until a few months later when she was working an evening shift. The nursing home was short-staffed and Penny found herself working the shift with just one other girl, Tracy, and the matron in charge. With one less member of staff, they were run off their feet, and Penny only had a chance to call in very quickly on Jane who had been ringing her buzzer every five minutes since she had started that evening. Trying to do several jobs at once, she dashed to Jane's room to see what was the matter.

Jane was paralysed from the waist down and so could not get herself out of bed. As Penny walked into her dimly-lit room, she smiled; Jane looked really cosy all tucked up in bed, ready to go to sleep. She seemed very sleepy as she opened her eyes on Penny's entrance. Penny noticed that her room was cool and so went over to the window to pull it shut, thinking that she had probably been ringing to complain that she was cold, but it was Penny who turned cold when she heard what Jane was about to say.

Jane drowsily explained to her that she was really tired and needed to get some sleep. Penny agreed that it was late and that she must be weary. Jane then continued by saying that although she had enjoyed the nice conversation she had just had with the little girl, she would like her to leave now. Penny was at first confused.

"What little girl?" she asked, as she tucked under the bedclothes at the bottom of her bed.

"The pretty one," Jane said, sounding a little frustrated, "the little girl with the blonde ringlets. She's lovely but I am really tired now and she must leave me to sleep."

Penny knew that no visitors had entered the premises that evening, and as it was after nine o'clock, it was unlikely that anybody would call at so late an hour. She froze as the recollection of Muriel's story flooded into her memory. Jane was of totally sound mind and Penny was deeply unsettled by her claim, but humoured her anyway.

"Well, I'll ask her to leave now and let you sleep, and if she comes back, why don't you try to ignore her to make her leave," Penny suggested, her body still icy at the thought of the ghostly child.

She pulled Jane's door tightly shut and tiptoed back along the narrow, creaky corridor to the winding staircase and made her way down to the staffroom, where Tracy and Matron were both sitting.

"You look pale, love!" Tracy exclaimed. "Are you okay?"

Penny stared at her and then started to smile.

"Yes," she shrugged, "it was just something weird Jane said, claiming a little girl was in her room or something, maybe she's losing it ..." she added quickly, trying to make light of what had just disturbed her, but her voice faded as she noticed the expressions on both women's faces drop.

Matron cleared her throat and sighed.

"Poor Jane ..." she whispered. "Let's hope it's not true this time."

Penny was startled.

"What do you mean?" she blurted out.

Matron and Tracy exchanged meaningful looks and then proceeded to explain how both of them had also heard a similar story to the one Muriel had told Penny about the little girl in the well, but the sad tale didn't end there. Apparently, it had become a kind of folklore in the home, that little Emily visited residents who were close to their own death, almost like a guardian angel. Practically all of the residents since Matron had worked there (some fifteen years) had referred to a small blonde girl, usually around the time their health dwindled.

"Did Jane really say that?" Tracy asked with some doubt. "I'd heard the rumours from the other girls, but I didn't believe them."

Penny also didn't like such a dark notion, so evaded her question and busied herself for the rest of her shift, trying to put the awful idea out of her mind.

It wasn't until she came back to work for the Christmas break that she noticed Jane's room was empty. Matron explained that a few things had changed since she had last been in work, including Jane's condition. She had been taken to hospital the week Penny had last spoken to her, just after she had told her about the blonde girl. Jane's health had deteriorated dramatically and she had never been well enough to come back to the home.

Worse still, as Penny stood in the kitchen extension and wiped away a tear, and Matron leaned over to pass her a tissue, she noticed a huge round crack in the floor tiles directly underneath the large wooden table. Another deathly chill flashed down her spine as she wondered if that could have been the outline of where the dangerous old well had once stood.

THE SCENTED LADY

Kit had never been a superstitious woman. She liked to believe in coincidence and sometimes let herself feel comforted by the thought of her deceased husband looking down on her from above, but really she dismissed supernatural possibilities as fanciful mumbo jumbo. That was until one afternoon when she visited her elderly aunt in Waterloo.

After cycling along the prom and over to her aunt's house, Kit chained her bike to the rusting iron gatepost. She enjoyed visiting her rather eccentric old aunt – her only living relative of that generation left, and although they were not particularly close, they always enjoyed a pleasant time together. Her aunt's house was practically falling apart; she lived alone and wasn't one for fussing around with housework or gardening. Scattered rows of untidy repotted plants littered the overgrown front yard. Kit stepped over the variety of chipped pots and tubs and rapped on the door, some flakes of paint flicking off the frame with the vibration of the knock.

As always, she was welcomed by a brief embrace and was ushered into the front room. Amongst the clutter a space had been cleared, and a teapot, two cups and saucers and a plate of french fancies were laid out on the table ready. The two of them whiled away the afternoon, chatting about what had been happening on the news, what Kit's children were up to, the usual catching up.

As the evening drew in, Kit decided it was time to leave; she did not fancy cycling back along the prom in the dark. The two of them were stood in the gloomy hallway, with only the gentle light from the table lamp in the corner to illuminate them, when Kit suddenly jumped, startled. She had seen a dark shadow on the upstairs landing that moved into her line of vision and then passed onwards into the darkness of the unlit landing.

She shivered.

"Errm, I will just use the toilet before I go ..." she stammered, not wanting to alarm her elderly aunt and curious to discover who the sly intruder was.

Kit made her way very cautiously up the steep staircase, each creak unsettling her further. She reached the landing and flicked on the light switch with a loud snap. The now illuminated landing was deserted. Kit then methodically checked every room and found, to her relief, that the entire upstairs of the house was empty. She was puzzled, surely her eyes had not been playing tricks on her, the distinct shape of a figure had definitely been on the landing.

Kit than noticed a very heavy scent in the air. It was almost intoxicating her as she stood there, stock still. The scent was thick and sweet – unlike anything Kit had ever smelt before and it seemed to waft over her in waves. The potency of the perfume then faded all at once, and was replaced by the familiar smells of her aunt's house: an immediately identifiable mixture of cooked food, dust and old linen.

Kit shrugged off the niggling worry, she thought to herself that she must have imagined the fleeting figure, although it had seemed so real. She popped to the toilet and went back downstairs to find her aunt still waiting for her in the hall. She was smiling faintly.

"You saw it, didn't you?" she asked quietly, her voice calm and without concern. Kit nodded. She realised that something strange had just occurred. "I like to think of it as a non-threatening presence ..." her aunt continued in a very matter-of-fact tone, her voice trailing into silence. She had nothing further to say about the presence. Kit embraced her aunt again, this time pulling her close. "Did you smell the lovely perfume?" her aunt whispered, "I call her the scented lady!"

Kit left the house, unsure of what exactly it was she had witnessed on the landing, but further mention of the ghostly vision never passed between the two of them after that strange day.

PHOTOGRAPHIC POLTERGEIST

According to the Occultists, there is more to photographs than we realise. They not only contain the image of a person, but they also contain some essence of the subject's soul. Shamans and witch doctors from many of the so-called primitive tribes of the world refuse to have their photograph taken because they believe that the camera is able to steal a part of the soul. It's easy to laugh at these superstitious beliefs, but there may be a grain of truth in the claim. Witches in the West and practitioners of Voodoo, use effigies of an enemy and snippets of their adversary's hair to harm them. Sometimes, just having the name of a foe was enough to harm him or her through the use of magic. A painting of a person was also occasionally used by the practitioner of the Dark Arts to cause injury or death by supernatural means.

When the exact image of a person became available through the science of photography – a science that Occultists say was once known to the ancients but subsequently lost – better results were achieved by the malevolent spell-casters. This idea of photographs having supernatural properties would throw some light on the following strange cases.

In 1994, a woman named Irene told me that she had experienced poltergeist phenomena at her home, centred on an old cupboard in her kitchen. The middle drawer of the cupboard flew across the kitchen into the hallway one afternoon, and the startling incident was witnessed by almost a dozen people who had just attended the funeral of Irene's grandmother. I inspected the contents of the drawer and found they included an old photograph album containing snaps of Irene's late grandmother, and several children. In the same drawer there was a reel of cotton thread, a small piece of purple card that held a collection of sewing needles, and a frayed cloth tape measure.

When I opened the photograph album, a colour photograph of an elderly man dropped out. Irene explained that this was a recent snapshot of her grandfather, William, who was now living in a retirement home. She had decided to put his photograph in the album – which she had only recently found in her late grandmother's bedroom. It had seemed fitting to put William's photograph in the old album, because, curiously, there were pictures of his late wife and her three younger sisters in the book, but there were no old pictures of William on any of the pages. Irene's grandmother had separated from her husband twenty years before, so Irene assumed that that was why her grandfather had not been included in the family album.

I had a strange hunch about this. I examined the photographs of the three children – whose ages ranged roughly from about nine to twelve – and noticed that two of them were upside-down. Irene was quite shocked to see that the pictures had been inverted. The photographs were mounted on the page by means of four, forty-five-degree slits, which received the corners of the snaps, so surely someone must have deliberately turned those photographs upside-down? No, they hadn't, as we soon learned.

The photographs were righted by Irene, and the snapshot of her grandfather was put back in what she considered to be its rightful place in the album. The album was then put back in the drawer, but on the following evening the cupboard shook violently and Irene watched as the drawer vibrated and gradually eased itself out of the cupboard until it clattered on to the floor. When she picked up the photo album, she discovered something quite shocking. Two of the sewing needles that had been attached to the piece of card, had now impaled the photograph of her grandfather William – through each of his eyes! What's more, the photographs of the three children were now missing from their page. Instead, they were on the front page of the album, loosely sandwiched together.

Irene visited her grandfather at the retirement home and told him about the strange goings on regarding the photograph album. The colour immediately drained from his face and he gasped for breath when he heard about the eerie episode. A couple of tears trickled from his eyes – he was visibly upset.

A week later, William's health suddenly deteriorated, and his condition quickly became so serious, that a priest was called in to administer the Last

Rites. Before his death, William asked to see Irene and, in a weak faltering voice, admitted to her that that he had once been a cruel bully to his wife's three sisters, who had been much younger than him. He had been twenty-five at the time and they had been aged eleven, twelve and fourteen. Through a set of tragic circumstances, the sisters had been forced to move in with Williams's seventeen-year-old wife – their eldest sister.

Further investigation revealed that William had raped the eldest of the three sisters after a drunken brawl and had almost blinded the youngest when he struck her viciously with the buckle of his leather belt in an unprovoked attack. The sharp buckle had almost ripped off the girl's eyelid. One of the girls died from meningitis, and the other two perished in a blaze that was allegedly caused by a carelessly-discarded cigarette at William's house. It was widely rumoured that William had deliberately caused the fire.

After listening to William's uncomfortable deathbed confession and researching into her family background, Irene was drawn to the weird conclusion that the poltergeist phenomenon might have started because some kind of essence contained in the photographs of the three sisters did not want to share the album with the snapshot of the hated brute who had made their lives hell.

PHOTO OPPORTUNITY

Another uncanny story involving a photograph took place back in the early 1980s.

In February 1981, twenty-seven-year-old Jayne Walker from West Derby, received a Valentine card from an admirer who later confronted her in the Philharmonic pub as she was enjoying a drink with friends. Her admirer was thirty-five-year-old Ronnie Saunders who was a bricklayer, and lived just a few streets away from Jayne. Ronnie had fallen for the petite red-head from the moment he had set eyes on her, and Jayne had had her eyes on the tall and stocky raven-haired Ronnie long before he had even noticed her.

The couple got on very well, and in May 1981, Ronnie took Jayne on a holiday to Paris, not just for the romance of it, but because Liverpool Football Club were due to play in the city against Real Madrid at the Parc des Princes stadium. Although she was an ardent Evertonian, Jayne attended the game with Ronnie. The final score was Liverpool 1, Real Madrid 0. A late goal by Alan Kennedy ensured that the trophy would remain in England for a fifth year. As the ecstatic Kop left the scene of the victory to the strains of *You'll Never Walk Alone*, Jayne and Ronnie went for a quick drink then headed back to their apartment at a hotel on the Rue de Saint Petersbourg.

In the hotel lounge, Ronnie got into a heated argument with a Spanish guest named Jorge Zorone, who had also just been to the match. He unwisely claimed that the Hungarian referee had shown favouritism towards Liverpool and that this had swayed the result. A diplomatic French guest at the hotel intervened and calmed down the Liverpudlian and the Spaniard, and Ronnie and Jorge ended up shaking hands and discussing sport in the hotel bar.

Although Jayne loved her boyfriend, she secretly thought that Jorge was the most handsome, athletic-looking man she had ever seen, and when she was introduced to the Spaniard, she felt a shiver of delight when he bowed, took hold of her hand and kissed her knuckles. His dark eyes had a twinkle of mischief and passion, and his smile had an innocent genuineness about it, which she found irresistible. He gallantly declared that Jayne was a perfect example of a beautiful English rose, and told a story about his grandfather, Vincent Zorone, a man who had won back the hand of his red-haired sweetheart after killing her lover in a fencing duel.

"Her hair was as red as yours, like a flame," Jorge said, grabbing a lock of Jayne's long hair and squeezing it in his fist as he grimaced, as if in pain.

At this, Ronnie decided that they had seen quite enough of Jorge for one night, and firmly took hold of his girlfriend's hand and told the Spaniard that he and Jayne were now going up to their room to get some much-needed sleep. Jorge seemed genuinely sad to see Jayne leave, and watched wistfully as Ronnie pulled her along after him as he went to the elevator. Jayne turned back, gazed dreamily at Jorge and gave him a feeble wave. The elevator doors parted and the English couple entered the lift, which took them to their room on the fifth floor. As it happened, Jorge Zorone's apartment was on the same floor, just four doors away down the corridor.

At four o'clock that morning, Jayne woke up after hearing a strange clicking sound and seeing a bright light momentarily flash through her closed eyelids. She awoke, and immediately the strong scent of Jorge's after-shave drifted under her nose. A voice next to her, somewhere in the darkness whispered: "Jayne, I love you. Come away with me."

Jayne recoiled with fright as Jorge's face suddenly loomed closely over her. She wondered about the click and the flash, and she groggily asked, "Did you take a photograph of me just now?"

"No, my darling. You must have dreamt it."

"Look, I don't know what you want, but if you don't get out of here this minute, I'll wake up Ronnie, and he'll knock you out," whispered Jayne between gritted teeth.

Jorge backed off into the darkness and silently left the apartment. Jayne was left wondering how Jorge had managed to gain access to the hotel room, and she felt creeped out by the whole episode, despite her earlier opinion of the handsome Spaniard.

On the following morning, Jayne decided that it would be wise to say nothing about Jorge's intrusion into the bedroom in the middle of the night, it would only cause an almighty row, and someone might end up getting hurt. However, curiously enough, and much to Jayne's relief, the lecherous Spaniard seemed to be making himself scarce at breakfast.

At around 10am, Ronnie and Jayne were just finishing packing their suitcases, when Ronnie cried out in agony and collapsed on to the bed. He writhed around on the bed and told Jayne that he felt very hot and was finding it difficult to breathe. The hotel manager was summoned, and he in turn called for a doctor. The doctor examined Ronnie, and confirmed that he was running an abnormally high temperature. He was obviously suffering from some kind of fever, but the doctor couldn't be sure what had caused it. He would need further tests, but since they were going home that night, the doctor advised seeking medical help when they got back home.

The strange thing was that the fever suddenly ceased after half an hour and Ronnie recovered from the strange condition with no ill effects.

Shortly after all this, Ronnie and Jayne were down in the foyer arranging for a taxi to take them to the airport later in the day, when the hotel manager began having a lively discussion in French with the assistant manager. Jayne knew a little French, and from her limited knowledge she could gather that the assistant manager was saying that a guest had stolen a number of keys to the different rooms. The police soon turned up at the hotel, and after talking to the manager, they rode the elevator to the fifth floor. Ronnie and Jayne went up to their own room about ten minutes later. As they passed Jorge's room, they noticed that the door was open, and they could hear the raised voices of two policemen, quizzing him over the keys he had in his possession. Jayne hung about in the corridor, staring in at Jorge and the police officers, determined to find out what was going on, but Ronnie urged her to stop being nosy.

Jayne was about to walk on, when she noticed something very strange which chilled her to the bone. Upon a table in the room, just by the door, was a candle which was slightly burned down, and in front of it there was a polaroid photograph of Ronnie – asleep in bed. Jayne immediately thought back to the nocturnal visitation by the creepy Spaniard. She had been convinced that she had heard a click followed by a flash of light which had penetrated her eyelids. It must have been been Jorge taking a picture.

Jayne was so outraged that she walked right into Jorge's apartment and tried her best to tell the policemen about the photograph and how the Spaniard had somehow gained access to her bedroom without their permission. Jorge cursed Jayne in his native tongue, and his attractive face seemed to be transformed with evil. The police inspected the photograph of Ronnie and noticed that it was singed in the centre by a candle flame. The photograph and candle stood upon a piece of paper upon which strange symbols had been scrawled all over it.

When Ronnie was shown the partly scorched snapshot, his blood ran cold, and he angrily asked Jorge, "What's your game, eh?"

But the police intervened before Jorge could reply.

The Spaniard was arrested for stealing several spare keys to rooms in the hotel and was soon led outside to a waiting police car and taken off to the station. The hotel manager had no idea what Jorge had been doing with the photograph, but Jayne was sure that he had been carrying out some sort of black magic ritual, using Ronnie's photograph to harm him. The way Ronnie had burned up with the mysterious transient fever led her to believe that it was Jorge who had inflicted the condition, through supernatural means. The Liverpool couple booked out of the hotel that evening and were only too glad to return home.

Be careful who you give your photographs to …

THE REVENGE OF MARTHA DUNN

In 1802, a Liverpool clipper ship named the *Martha Dunn* set sail from Havana to Liverpool, England, with a cargo of 200 hogsheads of rum and 700 sacks of cane sugar. The *Martha Dunn* was captained by William Benedict, a Liverpool-born mariner who had been reared in Pennsylvania.

The bond between a captain and his ship is well-known in maritime circles, but Captain Benedict's fondness for the *Martha Dunn* clipper was nothing short of a love affair. The captain frequently paced up and down the decks talking to his vessel, and on some occasions, he would affectionately stroke and pat the ship's bowsprit. The members of the crew were used to their captain's idiosyncrasies, and in a way, they also felt as if the ship had a personality of its own.

A fortnight after leaving Havana, the *Martha Dunn* sailed into Liverpool Bay in the middle of the night. A thick fog was hanging over the murky waters, and the lookouts could see virtually nothing. All they knew was that they must be near to the Wirral Peninsula.

Then one of the lookouts spotted a light flickering in the distance, and assumed that it was the beam of the Mersey lighthouse guiding them to their destination. The helmsman quickly changed course and Captain Benedict and his crew breathed a sigh of relief and assumed that they would soon be berthed at the Salthouse Dock, ready for a well-deserved drink in one of the city's many waterfront taverns.

Minutes after the helmsman had changed course, the rays from the lighthouse flickered, then died. Too late, Captain Benedict and the crew of the *Martha Dunn* must have realised that the light they had seen had probably come from the lantern of the ruthless men known as the 'wreckers'. On nights when visibility was poor, the infamous wreckers lured unsuspecting ships on to the treacherous rocks of the Wallasey coastline, by waving lanterns which the sailors mistook for the safety of a lighthouse.

Their evil trick certainly worked upon this foggy night, because the *Martha Dunn* smashed into the jagged rocks and almost capsized. Captain Benedict and all of the crewmen were thrown into the sea. Three of the crew drowned almost immediately, for, like many sailors of that time, they were unable to swim, and one man's back was fatally broken as he was hurled on to the rocks.

Only Captain Benedict and one member of his crew managed to swim to land, but as soon as they reached the pebbled foreshore, the exhausted men were viciously clubbed to death by one of the wreckers. Maritime law stated that a ship could not be legally salvaged if her captain, or just one of the crew survived, so the wreckers always made sure that there were no survivors.

The band of wreckers who murdered Captain Benedict and his crew belonged to a particularly callous and organised gang of men who were looked after by a notorious old woman known as 'Mother Redcap', who kept an inn of ill repute on the edge of Liscard Moor. Mother Redcap's inn provided a hiding place for the wreckers and smugglers of Wallasey; a place to stash their loot away from the eyes of the law and the customs officers.

Upon this still and fog-bound night, something very curious happened. As the wreckers rowed out towards the deserted *Martha Dunn*, ready to claim her cargo of rum and sugar, a wind suddenly started to stir. The strong breeze wafted away the thick fog and filled out the *Martha Dunn's* sails. As it did so, the clipper started to back off the rocks and righted itself once it reached the open water.

The frustrated wreckers in the lifeboat watched in amazement as the deserted ship sailed out to sea. They rowed furiously in an attempt to catch up with her, but it was no use; the *Martha Dunn* was picking up speed as the wind which had come from nowhere blew her into the darkness.

Henry Hargreaves, the evil man who had bludgeoned Captain Benedict and his crewman to death, cursed and raged as he watched his valuable prize disappearing before his very eyes into the night. He urged his companions in the lifeboat to keep on rowing after the derelict ship, but they refused, saying that the wind was too strong and the water too choppy.

At first light, Henry Hargreaves and five of his cronies spotted the *Martha Dunn* sailing erratically in the direction of Hilbre Island, off West Kirby, and they decided to take a small, single-masted fishing vessel out to the clipper, in a last attempt to salvage her. This proved to be a big mistake.

In full view of the crowds who had gathered on the shore to watch the salvage operation, the *Martha Dunn* suddenly performed a steady and seemingly controlled U-turn, as if someone was at her wheel. She then started to accelerate towards the fishing vessel. Henry Hargreaves looked on in sheer terror, as the *Martha Dunn* came careering past the fishing boat. Although it just missed hitting it by a matter of feet, the wake of the clipper almost swamped the tiny vessel, which was left violently rocking into the unsettled sea.

The two seamen with Hargreaves were quaking with fear and claimed that the *Martha Dunn* was a possessed ship. Terrified, they insisted that the chief wrecker return them to land. But Hargreaves was, above all else, a greedy man, and the thought of someone else claiming the clipper's valuable cargo was too much for him to bear. Hargreaves cursed his shipmates, calling them superstitious, yellow-bellied cowards. But minutes afterwards, the *Martha Dunn* was closing in on the fishing boat again, and this time she rammed it head on and cut right through the vessel, splintering her hull into matchwood. One of the wreckers died immediately in the collision, and the other one slowly bled to death in the water, with a long wooden splinter impaled in his neck. Henry Hargreaves clung desperately to a small, broken-off length of the fishing boat's mast, and listened to the grotesque gurglings of the doomed man. He also watched with relief as the accursed clipper drifted off into the early morning mist.

As soon as he felt that it was safe to do so, Hargreaves turned and started to swim for shore. He hadn't gone far when he noticed that the crowd on the shore were jumping up and down and roaring with excitement. The wrecker then glanced over his shoulder and was instantly seized with panic. The towering hulk of the *Martha Dunn* was almost upon him. Hargreaves was briefly heard to scream as the massive hull smashed into him. His bloated, broken body was later found on the sands of Hoylake, stinking and rotten, it had been half-eaten by the crabs and seagulls.

No one knows what happened to the *Martha Dunn*, but there were many strange tales about her fate.

According to one legend, when the body of Captain Benedict was being buried in a churchyard overlooking the sea near Neston, the deserted *Martha Dunn* came floating down the River Dee in full sail, and sank within sight of the startled mourners.

It was as if the derelict ship had decided to join her beloved captain in one last supreme act of loyalty ...

THE SATANISTS

In 1997, Martin, a former mortuary attendant, came down to the studios of Radio Merseyside to ask me to sign two *Haunted Liverpool* books. After I had signed the books, Martin told me a curious story that had happened to him some years earlier.

He told how, one night, a young man of about thirty-five years of age collapsed and was brought into casualty by ambulance, but died moments later. He had been accompanied by three people, all in their mid-twenties, and all dressed in black. They each wore silver pentacle talismans around their necks and were seemingly quite unperturbed by the death of their friend. They just stood there, expressionless, without uttering a word.

A post-mortem was carried out to determine the cause of death, as the man had not suffered from any known medical condition and had not had an accident of any kind. When the deceased man's clothing was removed, he too was found to have a large pentacle tattooed on his chest. At the centre of the tattoo there was a horned devil's head with a leering face. The only jewellery found on him was a plain silver ring on the third finger of his left hand. The coroner thought nothing of this ring at the time, simply making a note of it in his record book, but it was soon to become the centre of a bizarre and sinister incident.

The dead man was taken down to the mortuary, and was accompanied by his three eerily dressed companions who refused to leave the corpse, despite the protestations of the coroner and his staff. The creepy trio stood guard over their companion's corpse and advised the mortuary attendant not to remove the ring from his left hand, intimating that something terrible would happen to him if he were to take the silver band off. Martin felt uncomfortable and threatened by the weird threesome, and assured them that the ring would stay on the hand of their late colleague; he had no intention of taking it off.

However, when the dead man's friends had finally been persuaded to leave the hospital mortuary, Martin decided to remove the ring in order to take a closer look at it. Perhaps there would be some strange inscription on the inside. But the ring wouldn't budge, no matter how hard he pulled. By this time his curiosity had got the better of him, so he resorted to lubricating the troublesome finger with soap and water.

What took place next was to give Martin such a shock that it would effect his health for months afterwards. As he was starting to work the ring over the dead man's knuckle, the other hand suddenly shot up with lightning reflexes and grabbed the mortuary attendant's wrist in its icy grip.

Martin almost fainted with fright. He struggled to wrench himself free, but the dead man's fist held him fast in a vice-like grip. After several heart-stopping minutes, that seemed to last for an eternity, Martin managed to yank his hand free, and he bolted out of the mortuary with his nerves jangling. Once he was out of the building, he wandered about for a while in a stunned state, and eventually staggered to the nearest pub. With white face and trembling hands he leant against the bar and ordered a double scotch to calm his nerves.

Later that day he told his superiors that he felt ill and he was allowed home. When he reached his house he was suddenly overcome with an overwhelming tiredness and he took himself to bed. Martin's sleep was haunted by the terrifying memory of the icy, vice-like hand, and on the following morning, he telephoned his employers and claimed that his illness had worsened overnight. He was given the rest of the week off.

When he returned to the mortuary he tried to carry on as if nothing had happened, but his nerves were shot to pieces. To make matters worse, he was visited a number of times by the sinister people dressed in black, and with unsmiling faces, they warned him never to interfere in their matters again.

He didn't need to be told a second time!

SENTIMENTAL JOURNEY

Billy Marston had a very special knack for remembering things in great detail, because his work demanded it. A considerable part of his job as a painter and decorator was to work out estimates, and to then recall what materials would be required, and in what quantities and measurements, without the need to even note them down.

Billy remembers the date of the following strange incident quite clearly, in every detail, even though he was eighty-nine when he related his account of it to me.

It was Monday, 11 November 1974. Every newspaper, every radio and television news programme was full of the mysterious disappearance of the Earl of Lucan. The vanishing lord had abandoned the car he had used to flee from London at Newhaven on the south coast. Detectives had hoped to catch up with the Earl to determine whether he could help them with their inquiries into the 'Upstairs-Downstairs' murder of the Lucan children's nanny, and the attack on Lady Lucan.

The elusive Lord Lucan has still not been found to this day. Much was made of his vanishing act in the media at the time, and he became quite a household name.

As one mystery unfolded in London on that rainy November night, another one was about to commence two hundred miles further north in the Mossley Hill area of Liverpool.

At around 9pm, at a public house on Rose Lane called the Rose of Mossley, sixty-year-old bachelor Billy Marston, was lost in thought as he leaned at the bar, his cloth-capped head bowed over a half-empty glass of Mackeson stout. Billy was inwardly reminiscing about the past and, at the same time, worrying about the future. A painter and decorator by trade, Billy was increasingly finding that much younger men were being employed in the painting and decorating business and he was finding it hard to compete. Anyway, it wouldn't be long before he was drawing his old age pension. Where had all those years gone? What had happened to all his friends and relatives?

Once upon a time, many years ago, he used to go out on dates with attractive women, and had lots of friends and brothers and sisters. But, sadly, he was now the sole survivor of his family and most of his friends had gone away to other areas, lost touch with him, or died. His best friend Mulhearne had died suddenly a year ago from heart failure. It had been a terrible shock and made him feel old. Julia, the sister who had been closest to Billy since childhood, had died from cancer five years before that.

With a deep sigh, Billy drank the last dregs of his glass of stout, and said goodnight to the barman. He left the pub and wearily trudged down Rose Lane towards his home, the way he did most nights, back to his lonely and rather neglected house on Woodlands Road.

As Billy trudged along through the soft drizzle, a gloomy depression engulfed him as he contemplated the bleakness of his life. He began to wallow in self-pity, and felt his throat choking up with melancholy, when a man came walking out of a side street and startled him. In a low, professional-sounding singing voice the stranger sang a song which Billy hadn't heard for years. The song was *Sentimental Journey* and dated back to the 1940s. The first verse floated through the damp night air:

> *Gonna take a sentimental journey,*
> *Gonna set my heart at ease,*
> *Gonna make a sentimental journey*
> *To renew old memories.*

The stranger's youthful stride quickly put increasing distance between himself and Billy Marston, and in less than a minute, he was a fleeting figure, barely visible through the drizzle as he flitted up the lane. He could still be heard whistling the wistful melody as he melted into the shadows of a large oak tree's overhanging branches.

Billy slowed down, the words still ringing in his ears. He knew the song well and it had struck a chord in him.

"That sounds like a good idea," he muttered to himself, "I think I'll take a sentimental journey of my own."

His mood immediately lifted. He turned, and walked off in the opposite direction with a renewed sense of purpose. He had decided to revisit his old neighbourhood on Penny Lane. He was filled with the need to go on a sort of pilgrimage, to pay some homage to the golden years of his life. There are mental states of heightened alertness in the human mind of which we are hardly aware. The alpha, beta, delta rhythms of the mind as it sleeps, pays attention, or meditates, are fairly well known to neurologists, but this state of heightened consciousness was completely alien to Billy. It was almost euphoric, yet mystical.

As Billy reached the corner of Briardale Road and Penny Lane, he turned right, and as he did so, he made a turning back into into the world of 1929. The drizzle was suddenly no more and Billy felt as if he was fifteen again. Stiff joints, rheumatic twinges and eyes blurred by cataracts were no more, he felt sprightly, energised and fully alive. And bliss! The teeth in his mouth were his own again. The cloth cap had inexplicably vanished from his bald pate, to reveal a head of thick blonde hair.

He immediately noticed that the shops on the lane were the ones that had been there in the 1920s. The shops had all shut up for the night, but he noted all the old, familiar painted signs above their fronts. The old greengrocers, the bread and cake shop, the newsagent and tobacconist. Mrs Bruce, one of his aunt's neighbours, came down the lane. As she shuffled past him, she said, "You'd best be getting home, Billy. You young gallivanter."

Billy gazed at her in awe, but felt impelled to walk on, for he instinctively knew that if he was to allow himself to doubt that he was back in the late 1920s, for even one second, the spell would be broken and he'd find himself back on the rainy night-time street of 1974.

He walked on as if in a dream. The distinctive low moaning sound of a rolling tramcar brought a smile of recognition to Billy's face. It sailed into his view, rocking slowly from side to side up Smithdown Road: a tram with a ghostly, gas-lit interior. Shadowy figures were both seated and standing in its saloon, heading for the terminus. Cobbled roads stretched before him where macadam surfaces had lain in the dreary decade he'd left behind.

He crossed the road, hopping over tram lines worn shiny by a non-stop stream of trams ferrying their passengers to and from the city centre, and made his way to the home of his youth on Charles Berrington Road. He unbuttoned his overcoat and removed his scarf; it was a lovely warm evening and felt like summer. Downwind, on a gentle breeze, came the delightful, memory-jogging aroma of Ogden's mellow pipe tobacco. Two old men, Mr Godley and the meerschaum pipe-smoking Mr Greene, stood on their neighbouring doorsteps chatting, or 'chinwagging', as they used to call it back in the twenties. They were discussing Lancashire's recent win by ten wickets against South Africa at the three-day match at Liverpool Cricket Club, in Aigburth. Billy noted everything they said as he passed by.

Further up the road he passed old Mrs Brown's front parlour window and heard her playing a truly haunting melody on her old upright piano. It was Hoagy Carmichael's *Stardust*. In 1929 Billy had courted a beautiful girl named Violet who had loved that song. Filled with nostalgia, the music tugged at his heartstrings and he felt the full force of the emotions he had experienced at the time. He resolved to call at her home in a short while, just to hold her in his arms one more time.

Billy gazed up at the jewelled, velvety sky and whispered a few very apt lines which he had remembered from the song Mrs Brown was gently playing:

High up in the sky the little stars climb,
Always reminding me that we're apart,
You wandered down the lane and far away,
Leaving me a song that will not die.

A red-nosed drunk with a rakishly tilted bowler hat embraced the column of a lamp-post as he howled out *Old Man River* – shattering Billy's reveries about the stars and Violet and romance.

Billy paused as he approached the bay window of the front parlour he knew so well from long ago; the front parlour of his own old house, where he had lived until he was married at the age of twenty-two. An overwhelming sadness and emptiness suddenly came over him, damping down the euphoric rush that had so far accompanied his sojourn into the past. His poor, working-class mother and father and sisters lived at the house, and they had barely been able to scrape together a living in those hard times. Billy wished he could somehow convert all of his savings in 1974 into the currency of 1929 and stuff it through the letterbox in the front door. But that would only create a paradox.

Billy stood in the shadows, gazing at the house, afraid to knock on the front door he knew so well. He knew that if he entered that house, he would never be able to leave again. It would simply be too emotional to pay a flying visit, and something deep down told him that this stroll into bygone days was due to come to an end at any moment.

Then, suddenly, the front door opened.

Billy's heart thumped wildly inside his chest. His mother leant down and put the empty milk bottles out on the step. The family's old, one-eyed cat, Nelson, brushed past her legs and sauntered out into the street. The cat arched his back when he caught sight of Billy's stock-still silhouette lurking outside the lamp-post's fringe of illumination.

"Mum…" the faint word barely escaped from Billy's choked-up throat and drifted into the night air unheard by his beloved mother.

The door closed and Billy heard the sound of a bolt being drawn inside. He looked down at his old cat and bent down to reach out to him saying, "Nelson. Here, puss. Do you know who I am?"

The cat hissed and ran off into the night.

Billy silently said goodbye to the house and reluctantly walked away with scalding tears cascading down his cheeks. He stopped on Heathfield Road, and once again, his emotions were in turmoil. He stared at the upstairs window of Violet's bedroom. He knew that his first love was sleeping there, unaware of everything. The thought of tossing a handful of gravel at the window crossed his mind, but he knew that he had no right to confuse her – he must leave her be.

A policeman was approaching on his beat along Smithdown Road. It was time to leave.

"I will always love you, Violet," Billy whispered, eyeing the drawn curtains behind which his eternal sweetheart lay sleeping. He could almost hear her singing the words of *Stardust* in his mind.

Violet would die from a brain tumour in three years time …

Billy sorrowfully retraced his steps back up Penny Lane, until he reached the corner where his amazing journey into the past had begun. He knew that he couldn't stay in the past, and silently accepted the fact without protest. He was too upset to object. Whenever he had reminisced publicly about the good old days, people had told him he'd been looking at the past through rose-tinted spectacles, but now he knew that he hadn't. Now he knew exactly what he had lost – those carefree, halcyon days when his greatest worry had been what to wear on his dates with his sweetheart, Violet.

As Billy walked up Briardale Road, the stiffness of old age gradually returned to his joints and limbs, rheumatism became evident once again in his shoulder, and his vision clouded over once more, as the cataracts covered his eyes. A modern car sped past, then another – gone were the virtually car-free streets of the 1920s. He had returned to 1974 and the noise and bustle of the busy streets around Penny Lane made him feel dizzy and confused.

When Billy arrived home he sat in silence for a while, going over and over the night's events in his head. He could not be sure that he wasn't going mad. How on earth, and for what reason, had he been allowed to go back over forty years to the 1920s? It was a question to which he never found the answer.

On the following morning, right out of the blue, Billy was visited by a cousin with whom he'd lost touch, called Andy. Andy had travelled from St Helens specifically to find Billy, and admitted that his motivation for seeking him out had been loneliness, because he no longer had any immediate family around him. They had all died, one by one, leaving Andy completely on his own in the world. He had then remembered his cousin who was about the same age as himself.

Perhaps because they were both in the same situation, Billy and Andy got on famously and chatted into the small hours about incidents from their childhood and early lives. Here was a real life link with the past, thought Billy. It turned out that they still had a great deal in common; so much so, in fact, that Billy soon invited his cousin to live with him, and they made a pact to create and build a proper social life for themselves.

They started by paying a visit to the local crown green bowling club. Not only did they both enjoy the game and find that they were good at it, but they also met two women who took them off to ballroom dancing classes. Lonely nights and self-imposed isolation became a thing of the past for the two cousins and suddenly their old age did not seem so bleak after all. As an added bonus, all the exercise seemed to help Billy's rheumatism, and his painful, creaking joints eased.

Shortly after relating his touching timeslip tale to me, Billy Marston passed away, aged eighty-nine. He struck me as a very honest and straightforward man, and he earnestly assured me that the trip into the past really did take place, but he was at a loss to explain why or how it happened. What is apparent is that that night appeared to be a turning point in Billy's life, and from that time onward, he seemed to find his way again.

A SOLDIER'S RETURN

One stormy winter's night in January 1919, thirty-year-old Rose Griffith was sitting in the front parlour of her house in the vicinity of Newsham Park, playing an old seventy-eight record of *Roses of Picardy* on her horned Decca gramophone.

Rose was passionately singing along to the crackling record. She knew all the words off by heart:

> *Roses are shining in Picardy,*
> *In the hush of the silvery dew,*
> *Roses are flowering in Picardy,*
> *But there's never a rose like you!*

Rose's cousin Margaret turned up at the house that night. She was concerned about her cousin's increasingly eccentric behaviour, which had started when Rose had learned that her husband Ivor had been killed during the Battle of the Somme, three years before. That battle, which started on 1 July 1916 and ended on 13 November of that year, had been the bloodiest episode of the First World War, involving 1,353,000 troops representing thirty-five nationalities.

The great River Somme winds its way from the centre of Picardy to the Channel coasts, and even today, the name of the area remains a byword for futile and indiscriminate slaughter.

Margaret had heard about Rose's strange behaviour from neighbours in her street in Kensington. They had told her how Rose always left her back yard gate and back-kitchen door open, as she expected her late husband to come home any day. Before the war, he had always come through those doors when he returned home from work, and Rose claimed that, even after death, her deceased husband had returned several times to see her, and he had entered the house via the back yard and back-kitchen doors.

Rose looked a sorry state. Dark circles ringed her sad, sunken eyes, and when she sat talking about her beloved dead husband, she would wring her hands and rock slightly backwards and forwards. It was obvious that her thoughts were focused solely on her husband and she would repeatedly glance at the parlour door with an expression of expectation, as if she thought that Ivor was about to enter at any moment.

Margaret tried to talk some sense into Rose. She brewed a pot of tea and whilst she was in the back-kitchen, she attempted to close the door, as it was freezing cold and the open door was chilling the whole house. But, without saying a word, Rose immediately walked into the kitchen and opened it again.

"Look, Rose, Ivor will not be coming home tonight, tomorrow, or ever again," Margaret said quietly, gently taking her cousin's hand.

Rose was still looking past her and towards the back-kitchen door. She answered her cousin very calmly. "No, you're wrong, Margaret," and as Margaret silently embraced her, Rose quietly added: "He still comes to see me."

Margaret shook her head, she could see that she would have a very difficult job convincing Rose that the best thing would be to try and forget the awful loss of her husband and try to get on with her life. The two women sat in the parlour drinking tea for the remainder of that evening, and the storm outside showed no signs of abating. Rain and wind swept into the back-kitchen and Margaret drew nearer to the living room fire in an attempt to keep warm, whilst Rose remained oblivious to the rising chill and disruption in the room. Thunder rolled and lightning flashed through the scarlet parlour blinds.

At 11pm, suddenly Rose started humming a tune. She rocked back and forth in her chair, gazing vacantly into the dying embers of the coal fire. She then began to sing.

"Roses are shining in Picardy, in the hush of the silvery dew," her eyes were bright and sparkling as she sang to the dwindling flames.

Margaret sighed and bit her lip. It was almost unbearable to watch Rose suffering so badly and she decided that it was time that she left, as there was nothing she could do to alleviate her misery; her cousin seemed beyond help. She was just putting on her coat and hat when there was a distant thump from the rear of the house. It sounded like the back yard door being slammed shut – probably by the gales. Then there came another slamming sound. This time there was no mistaking it – the back-kitchen door had just been closed. Rose immediately stopped singing and jumped to her feet.

"Darling!" she exclaimed, a wide grin spreading across her illuminated face.

Margaret watched her cousin's reaction to the noises and was alarmed. She felt distinctly uncomfortable as her concern for her cousin increased.

The sound of heavy footsteps coming up the passage outside made Margaret jump to her feet too. The tread of boots came right up to the parlour door, and the knob of that door squeaked as it slowly turned. The two women stood transfixed, scarcely daring to breathe.

The door opened, and by the pale luminescence of the glowing gas mantle, they beheld the figure of a soldier, dressed in a mud-spattered British Army uniform, and looking weary and dejected, as if he had just emerged from the trenches. The figure stepped forward across the threshold of the parlour, and as he did so, Margaret let out a scream of absolute terror, because she could now clearly see that the soldier's face was gruesomely disfigured. Parts of his face were missing. There was a jagged, yawning black socket where his left eye should have been, and a section of exposed jaw and missing teeth on the lower side of his face, completed the horrendous picture.

Rose did not seem to be aware of the soldier's horrific injuries and stepped forward to embrace the terrifying apparition of what she obviously recognised as her husband. Margaret threw her hands up in fear and covered her face as she dashed past the ghostly soldier. She ran through the hallway and left through the back door. She ran out into the bleak back alley in the lashing rain without daring to even look behind her.

From that evening onwards and for the rest of her life, Margaret refused to go back to the house near Newsham Park.

LADY ON THE LEDGE

There is a block of inner-city apartments in Liverpool that was completely renovated in the late 1990s, changing it from one of those hard-to-let properties, into one of the most desirable addresses in the city. When the luxury dwellings became available, they were soon snapped up by young, upwardly mobile people keen to get on the property ladder and secure a trendy apartment for themselves in the city. However, neither the landlord, nor the unsuspecting new residents, knew about the eerie ghost that haunts the building.

The first realisation that something supernatural was at large occurred one night in 1999, when a professional couple, Greg and Susannah, were watching television in the lounge with all the lights switched off. The time was 9.45pm, and the only lights that illuminated the apartment, apart from the flickering television screen, came up from the sodium street lamps in the road below, filtered through the vertical blinds.

"What was that just then?" asked Greg.

He jumped up from the sofa, and stood stock still and wide-eyed, gazing at the window.

"What was what?" Susannah asked, staring at the same window in the hope of finding some kind of clue as to what he was going on about.

"Someone just walked past that window outside. It was a woman. She must be on the ledge," Greg gasped, and he cautiously parted the silver vertical blinds and peered through.

"You what?" Susannah said, unable to hide the doubt in her voice, as the apartment was five storeys up. "How could there be anyone out there. The ledge is too narrow to walk on. They'd be killed."

A narrow ledge, which was, in fact, just about big enough to walk on, did run around the building, but why would anyone risk their life walking along it at night?

"There's someone out there! Look!" said Greg, getting increasingly exasperated with his partner's attitude.

He tried to open the window to give the suicidal ledge stroller a piece of his mind, but Susannah always kept the double-glazed windows locked. As Greg went to fetch the key, Susannah also saw a young woman in black walking past the window. Her face was extremely pallid, almost blue, and her eyes looked dark and sad. On her head she wore a ladies' 1930s-style hat with a velvet pleated drape and bow. She also wore a black jacket and a calf-length shirt – not the sort of clothes to go climbing the outside of buildings in. She was bare-footed, and she walked slowly and deliberately along the narrow ledge without even acknowledging Susannah's presence.

As soon as Susannah set eyes on the lady in black she felt there was something ethereal and other-earthly about her. Greg returned with the key and quickly unlocked the handle on the window. He swung open the window and gazed along the ledge just in time to see the woman jump off the ledge. Greg recoiled from the window in shock, the vision he had just seen indelibly printed in his mind. He expected to hear a sickening crunch as her body smashed into the pavement below, but he heard no such sound.

As the colour drained from his face, he told Susannah what he had just witnessed, and she became very agitated. She suspected that the woman was actually a ghost, and her hunch proved to be right.

As Greg ran downstairs to check if the woman had fallen to the pavement, the same figure walked past the window once more and this time looked in at Susannah, who screamed and ran out of the flat as fast as her feet would carry her. She was so terrified that she ran down the five flights of stairs in her bare feet. On reaching the pavement outside she flung herself into Greg's arms, and the two of them stood there looking totally bemused.

The woman in black was neither there, nor up on the ledge. The ghost was later seen by several other people in the same block of apartments, and the same terrible scenario was played out before their eyes. Then, for some reason, the ghostly female made herself scarce for several months.

To this day, no one is certain who exactly the ghost walking the ledge and repeatedly jumping off it could be.

A woman named Theresa, who lives on the fourth floor of the apartment block said that on one occasion she actually saw a woman's body plunge past her window. Perhaps the suicidal shade is the ghost of someone who took her own life from the ledge of that building in the 1930s, but, up to press, I can find no record of such a suicide from that period.

Because of strained nerves after the experience, Susannah and Greg left their apartment and moved into less trendy, but much more congenial accommodation in Woolton village. The ghostly lady apparently still walks precariously on the ledge and then jumps to her 'death', and was seen as recently as March 2002.

A Cabbie's Tale

It was Autumn 2002 and just another November night on the taxi rank for Mike, a cab driver with over twenty years' experience of the hackneys. His cab was parked in the rank on Bolton Street, which runs from Copperas Hill and the north side of the Adelphi Hotel, to Skelhorne Street and Lime Street Station. Business was slow, and Mike chanced going to fetch himself a cup of hot black coffee from the café that caters for cabbies, situated just thirty feet away. Then Mike returned to his well-kept vehicle, and climbed into the driver's seat. He was just about to remove the safety lid from the polystyrene coffee cup, when he noticed a tall, gaunt-looking man in a long dark coat approaching from the direction of Lime Street Station.

Mike's cab was second in the queue of hackneys lined up in Bolton Street, and as the man crossed Skelhorne Street in his approach to the rank, the cab in front of Mike moved off. Mike gave up on his coffee and placed the cup in a holder on the dashboard. The man in the long black coat seemed to glide up to the vehicle in a most unnatural way, and what's more, he seemed to be muttering to himself. At closer quarters, the man looked about fifty-something, yet fleet-footed and agile. As he entered the cab, he said to himself, "I didn't quite get that."

"What was that, mate?" Mike asked, assuming the fare was talking to him.

The man impatiently waved his hand, dismissing Mike's query as a trivial distraction.

"That's all I need," Mike thought, an eighteen-carat nutcase talking to himself. "Where to, mate?"

The man looked up and closed his eyes for a moment, then in a deep, rich sounding voice he said, "Clubmoor. Yes, that's it, driver. Take us to Clubmoor!"

Mike wondered who the 'us' the well-spoken man was referring to could be. "Clubmoor? Er, what part of Clubmoor, sir?" he queried.

"I'll tell you soon, bear with me," was the passenger's strange reply.

Mike wondered whether it was worth starting the journey and took him to task.

"What do you mean, 'bear with you'? What's the address?"

Mike swung round in his seat and glared at the man.

His creepy passenger scowled back at him. "Look, driver, I don't expect you to understand what I am about to tell you …"

"Don't call me driver; it's Mike; and why wouldn't I understand? Go on, try me," Mike said, his patience visibly thinning.

"Very well …" the man leaned forward, ready to explain. "I have just come by train from Manchester. I am a medium, and I was in the middle of a séance when it was interrupted by a spirit with some urgent information. The information it imparted was vague and incomplete, but my spirit guide is helping out now."

Mike gave a blank look and uttered, "Oh, I see."

The man continued, "My name's Justin, and I swear every word I tell you is true. My guide, Augustus, is sitting next to me now, and all this is a matter of life and death."

Mike detected an air of sincerity in the man's voice which made him believe that he was not some crackpot after all. Mike had been feeling bored anyway on the quiet taxi rank, so he decided to give this adventure a whirl.

"Okay, Justin. I'll drive to Clubmoor and you can tell me what what's-his-name tells you."

"It's Augustus," said the psychic, urgently. "He's a bit faint tonight. He says Clubmoor and he is showing me a name with the word 'ash' in it. It's a street in Clubmoor. It could be Ashmont or Munash – it's a bit vague I suppose."

"Monash Road is in Clubmoor …" Mike said, gazing in his rear-view mirror as he turned up Skelhorne Street.

"That's it – Monash, and I even have the number on the door," Justin said with a smile. "Driver – I mean Mike – a woman's life may depend on this. It's a rather long-winded story, but in short, the woman is an old flame of mine, and the spirit of a relative of hers broke in on the séance to say that her life was in danger. A man with a knife is watching her."

Mike cursed the red traffic light under his breath, then sighed as he realised that he hadn't reset the meter.

"Man with a knife?"

The medium seemed deep in prayer with his hands clasped together and his eyes closed tightly. He didn't say anything for almost five minutes.

Mike pushed his vehicle to the limits and made Monash Road in record time.

"Here we are, mate."

Justin sprang from the cab and scanned the numbers of the doors until he came to the numeral which had been relayed into his mind by Augustus. He called at that address, and waited. He could hear someone moving behind the door, and he could see the tiny point of hallway light – just visible through the wide-angle door-viewer – blink off.

"Mary it's me – Justin! Open the door!" said the medium.

He heard the sounds of a chain being unfastened, and of a bolt being drawn back.

The door opened, and there was Mary, a woman Justin had not set eyes on for over a decade. When she broke off their romance, the sensitive medium had almost been destroyed by the heartbreak. Tonight she stood there gazing at him in surprise with a slight smile as she recognised him.

"Justin!" she gasped, stepping back into the hallway and invited him in.

Justin turned to the cab driver and called, "I won't be a moment."

Mike nodded, and waited. He sipped his now lukewarm coffee and shook his head, grinning at the extremity of the unusual tale he had been told so far.

Then there came an insistent tapping on the cab window. Mike turned, startled, to see a man of about thirty standing there. His head was shaven and his eyes had an intense, unsettling stare.

"Who was that man who just went in to Mary's place?" he demanded.

"I don't know, mate. Why?" Mike replied.

"I'm her husband – that's why, mate," said the man, who was obviously very agitated. Suddenly he produced a hunting knife, then turned to stare at the front door of Mary's home. "She's always bringing men back and it's got to stop," he said, to himself rather than to Mike.

As soon as the man moved away from the cab, Mike lost no time in calling the police on his mobile, as he felt a dangerous domestic incident was about to unfold.

Within ten minutes the police were at the scene, and the knifeman, who was pacing up and down outside Mary's house, fled when he saw them arrive, but he was soon caught on Queens Drive.

It turned out that Justin's supernatural tip-off had been correct. For over two months, Mary had been stalked by a man who had convinced himself that he was married to her. The stalker had a history of being obsessed with women, but had only ever been cautioned. Mary was amazed at the way Justin had turned up at her address through information imparted by a spirit. It had been the spirit of her uncle, who had always watched over her in life, and who was now apparently doing so in death as well.

Justin paid Mike for the unusual trip to Clubmoor, and told him that he would be staying with Mary overnight to calm her nerves. He would try his utmost to persuade his former love to move with him to Didsbury on the outskirts of Manchester.

A week later, coincidentally – or perhaps there were mysterious forces of synchronicity at work again – Mike and his wife went to the Puschka restaurant on Rodney Street to mark their tenth wedding anniversary. Moments after their arrival, Justin and Mary entered and were escorted to a table near the window. Justin spotted Mike and his wife, and he came over to say hello to them. He then returned to his table. As Mike and his wife were getting ready to leave the restaurant later that night, Justin came over and told the hackney driver that he would soon be hearing the patter of tiny feet.

"No way," Mike said.

He explained that he and his wife had been trying for children for so many years with no success. But, sure enough, three months later, Mike's wife discovered that she was pregnant. The couple were overjoyed.

SOMETHING BLACK

A premonition went unheeded with tragic results on 20 October 1966, when a nine-year-old Welsh girl, Eryl Mai Jones, told her mother that she had experienced a strange dream in which she had gone to school, only to find that the building was not there an more.

"Something black had come down all over it," the child told her mother.

Had she been more specific, her mother might have thought twice about sending her daughter to school the next day, because there certainly was 'something black' in their village; something which loomed darkly over them all and dominated the village landscape.

On the very next day, Eryl set off to her school in the Welsh mining village of Aberfan.

"Hurry now, mind you don't get soaked," shouted her mother.

On the way, she passed the enormous slag heap which had been there ever since she could remember, standing out starkly, like some malignant intruder, against the lush green Welsh hillsides surrounding the village. She paid it no attention; it had become part of the landscape, an ugly reminder of the vast dark labyrinth of coal tunnels which criss-crossed the ground deep beneath her feet, in which her father, and those of all her friends, worked their long and dangerous shifts.

She splashed along, avoiding the puddles which dotted the pavement; it had been raining incessantly for what seemed like weeks. When she reached the school she dashed under the shelter to join her friends.

Later that day, a black silent river of coal waste – half a million tons – slithered down the side of that enormous slag heap, engulfing the school and many adjacent homes. The choking black slag relentlessly forced its way in through doors and windows, killing one hundred and thirty-nine people, most of them children.

The terrible tragedy shook the whole nation and Mrs Jones soon learned that her little Eryl was among the dead. In fact, very few children in Aberfan survived the tragedy, and those who did had to live their lives in a village which had been plunged into silence – robbed of the sound of children's laughter.

THE DOOR

In this age of emails and the internet, I regularly receive many tales from Liverpudlians who have settled in other countries. This tale from the United States also took place in the 1970s, and was related to me by Susannah Rye, who left Liverpool with her husband in 1974 to live in Belwood, Illinois.

In 1976, Susannah was getting ready for bed one moonlit summer night. She carried the family cat Sydney down from her daughter's bedroom and was about to put it out when she saw something, which gave her palpitations. Through the pane of glass in the front door she saw a man and a woman outside on the porch. The man was very tall and broad with a shock of white hair and the woman was very small and delicate, and was wearing horn-rimmed glasses. The man had his large, chubby hands around the woman's throat, and he was shaking her like a rag doll as he throttled the life out of her. The fur on the cat's back stood up on end and it darted back up the stairs like a streak of lightning. Mrs Rye quickly followed in the cat's footsteps. She ran up the stairs two at a time to her husband and breathlessly gasped out the story about the strangler downstairs on the porch. Mr Rye telephoned the police and then, in typical American fashion, he removed his .38 revolver from his gun cabinet, ready to protect his family.

When the police arrived, they found no trace of the white-haired strangler, or his alleged victim, and for some strange reason, they seemed very subdued and uneasy as they listened to Mrs Rye's description of the people she'd seen on the porch. One of the policemen patted her on the shoulder, and after a long silent pause, he said: "Those people you saw, Mrs Rye; they weren't real."

Mr Rye was angry that the police were not taking his wife seriously and asked the policeman for an explanation.

The policeman awkwardly fidgeted with his hat and replied: "Well, sir. About three years ago, before you folks moved into this house, the people living here saw the same thing – a tall, well-built man with white hair, strangling a very small woman on the front porch. There was also a real murder here in 1966. A local mechanic strangled his wife. He was a big burly man with white hair. And she looked like the lady your wife described – petite, like a little bird. The murder happened five miles down the road from here."

"If that's the case, then why should we see their ghosts here? Why have they singled out this house?" asked Mr Rye, reluctant to believe such an extreme tale.

The policeman said that the front door of the Rye's house had once been the front door of the mechanic's house. The landlord had salvaged the door when the strangler's house was burnt down by a lynch mob. The door, which was very attractive – being very old and elaborately carved wood – was later used to replace the door of the house now lived in by the Rye family.

The policeman's story made the Ryes' skin crawl. Mr Rye lost no time in taking the jinxed front door off its hinges and replaced it with a new one. He offered the old door to his neighbour, Dave Reichart, who had no belief in anything of a supernatural nature.

Dave left the door in his back garden, intending to use it as his front door but never quite getting round to hanging it. Three years later, he reported seeing ghostly figures in the glass panes of that same door. Dave, his wife, and his US Marine brother, Mike, briefly saw the eerie figures of a man strangling a woman.

In 1983, the ghostly scene was re-enacted yet again in the glass panes of the door, but the new residents of the house, who were born-again Christians, smashed the door up and shattered its panes.

Backpackers' Nightmare

Another tale from America was reported to me by a former Liverpool John Moores University student called John, who now lives in Los Angeles.

In 2002, before he emigrated to America, John travelled across the United States with his friend Rob. In the autumn of that year, John and Rob were camping deep within the pine forests that lie huddled around the pristine foothills of the Ouachita Mountains in South-western Arkansas. A full moon hung overhead, and the two young men sat around their camp fire, chatting about the day's events. Twinkling in the distance were the lights of the small college town of Arkadelphia, which has a population of about ten thousand, and is the epitome of small town America. In the opposite direction the cliffs lining the Ouachita River were clearly visible, with the moon reflected in the quietly flowing waters far below.

Upon this autumnal night, shooting stars rained from the sky, and while John and Rob looked up in wonder at the heavens to take in the celestial fireworks, they both heard the faint sound of someone sobbing, somewhere in the distance. The crying did not come from the direction of the town – it came from somewhere deep in the forest. About a minute later, the two young men heard a faint rustling sound approaching. A figure darted past them. By the flickering light of the camp fire, they saw that it was a woman dressed in a long black dress. Covering her face was a black veil, and as she moved along she bowed her head as she sobbed.

The young men followed her from quite a distance, as they suspected that there was something sinister about the sobbing night stroller. The woman in black walked for some ten minutes, and John and Rob followed her to the edge of a cliff overlooking the river. They soon realised what the eerie woman's intention was. She looked up at the moon – then jumped! John and Rob watched in horror as her body hit the rocks below – and then seemed to evaporate into thin air. Not even the faintest splash was heard. The men looked at one another in horror and disbelief, then rushed back to their car and drove over seventy miles to another spot where they could rest for the night, but they got little sleep, because neither could stop thinking about the ghostly woman they'd seen.

On the following day they talked to people in the area about the suicidal shade, and were told that the place where they had seen the ghost was haunted by an apparition known as the Lady in Black. It was said to be the restless ghost of a young woman named Jane, who had been a student at Arkadelphia's Ouachita Baptist University in the 1920s. The students of Ouachita University had always competed with the students of Arkadelphia's other acclaimed university – Henderson. It was unheard of for any students from these two universities to mingle socially, and in the 1920s, Jane, from Ouachita University, began to date a young man named Joshua, a student of Henderson State University.

Unfortunately, Joshua's friends held the same prejudices as the rest of the population, and soon began to ostracise him and threatened to never speak to him again if he didn't end his romance with Jane. Joshua eventually succumbed to the pressure, and broke up with Jane on the night of the annual homecoming dance at Henderson. The girl was inconsolable. Her friends tried to tell her that it was for the best, but she pushed past them all and ran away in floods of tears. Her friends became very concerned about her emotional state.

Jane ran up to her dorm room, where she put on a black dress and a veil which she had recently worn at a relative's funeral – then headed for the steep cliffs over the Ouachita River, where she could put an end to the intense, unbearable heartbreak of the break-up with Joshua. She had decided that she could not live without him.

Not long after her suicide, Jane's ghost was seen hurrying to the place of her death by many people in the area, including Joshua. The ghost of the Lady in Black has also been seen haunting the campus of Henderson State University – looking for her lost love. They say her ghost still walks to this day.

When John and Rob heard the story of the Lady in Black, they understandably shuddered. The figure had seemed so lifelike, so real, as carnate ghosts often do.

HOT GOSSIP

In the village of West Derby, in the late nineteenth century, there were four women who had remained good friends since their childhood days. They were Emily Titherington; a red-haired greengrocer, Miss Jessie Moore; a tall and elegant young lady who worked as a draper, the beautiful, angelic-faced Henrietta Colquitt; dressmaker, and Miss Alice Crosby, amusingly described by her three peers as a wealthy loafer. Miss Crosby had never worked since leaving school at the age of fourteen, and had no need to seek employment at all, as she had inherited quite a fortune from her uncle at the age of twelve. However, her mother owned a newsagents and Alice occasionally helped her behind the counter, more for her own amusement than anything else.

All four women were highly regarded as pillars of the community, but behind closed doors, above Emily's shop on Wednesday evenings, the quartet of young ladies let down their hair to smoke, drink and play poker – in between catching up on the rumours and gossip traversing West Derby's grapevine. During the girls' talk one Wednesday evening, the greengrocer Emily Titherington mentioned a minor mystery that was lapped up and discussed by her friends.

Apparently, a stranger had started coming into her shop on a fairly regular basis to purchase lemons. He sometimes bought apples and oranges, but each week, for three weeks, he had purchased six lemons at Emily's shop. Alice asked her friend to describe this man. Emily said he had light-brown hair, was very tall, aged about forty, and had a comical turned-up moustache. He spoke with a strange accent which she couldn't place.

"That's Mr Glossop," declared Alice, puffing on a Three Castles cigarette. "He comes into Mama's shop for the *Daily Telegraph* each morning. He's very handsome."

Jessie Moore sipped her Gordon's Gin and rolled her eyes knowingly as she noted the look of infatuation blossoming on Alice's face. She delicately licked her lip and asked Alice what else she knew about the newcomer to the village.

Alice shrugged and said that no one knew where Mr Glossop was from. Her mother was curious about his background too. Emily Titherington said she felt that he held some dark secret.

"Call it intuition perhaps," the greengrocer said, "but I have uncanny feelings about Mr Glossop."

Without looking up from her poker hand, Henrietta Colquitt said: "Do you mean to say, Emily, that you have never politely asked Mr Glossop about his accent?'"

"No I have not," Emily replied.

"How do you know the man's surname?" Henrietta asked.

"He reserves his copy of the *Telegraph* and that's the name Mama writes on his newspaper," Alice told her, and she added that Mr Glossop preferred to pick up his newspaper personally rather than have it delivered to his address.

"I wonder what he does with all those lemons?" Emily mused.

On the following day, a smart-looking, tweed-suited Mr Glossop came into the newsagents to pick up his copy of the *Daily Telegraph,* and Alice Crosby was present. She handed the newspaper to him and quietly mentioned that she could not place his accent. Mr Glossop said that it was Cornish; he hailed from St Ives. He smiled, nodded politely and left the newsagents. As soon as he was outside the shop, Glossop began to search intently through the pages of the newspaper. He always did that, whereas most customers carried their newspapers home to be read in private.

By the following Wednesday, when the four young ladies met again in the room over Emily's shop, Henrietta had managed to discover two things about the Cornishman from her brother-in-law, the local postman who had delivered a letter to Mr Glossop. Mr Glossop's first name was Augustus, and he lived at Runnymede Cottage, an old dwelling near Sandfield Park that had lain empty for years before he took up residence. Alice told them that she had spoken to Mr Glossop and he had told her that he was from St Ives in Cornwall. Alice added that she had noticed a peculiar habit of the Cornishman. She explained about his frantic scanning of the newspaper as soon as he bought it, as if he was looking for something of great personal importance among the columns and articles.

Emily's contribution to the gossip was that Mr Glossop had been to her shop to buy apples and grapes, but that he hadn't purchased a single lemon. However, she had noticed something rather peculiar; Mr Glossop's once light brown hair now verged on being blond.

"That's it! Of course!" Jessie Moore said, pointing a finger at Emily. "My mother used to do that. Lemon juice can lighten hair – it's a natural dye."

Henrietta touched the tip of her chin with her index finger and began to meditate on all of the strange facts concerning Augustus Glossop.

"Mm, lemon juice. I do believe that our Mr Glossop is trying to alter his appearance for some reason. I think he's got something to hide."

"Do you think he may be a murderer on the run?" Alice asked with a worried look.

"It's quite possible," Jessie replied, encouraging the suspicion. "Perhaps that's why he looks through the newspaper so eagerly. Perhaps he is checking to see if the police are on to him."

"Then perhaps *we* should go to the police ourselves," Alice suggested.

"There isn't one iota of evidence to prove anything," said Henrietta, pouring cold water on Alice's idea, but she then made a constructive suggestion. "Perhaps we should check the newspapers though, to see if there is anything relating to a Mr Glossop, or a recent murder committed in Cornwall."

Each day, Henrietta Colquitt purchased the *Daily Telegraph* and scrutinised every page and article, looking for any news of a Cornish murderer on the run. After almost a week of searching, she came across a very curious article that concerned the mysterious disappearance of a forty-two-year-old Lanyon Tregelly, from Boscastle in Cornwall. Two months previously, in July, Mr Tregelly had gone swimming off the Cornish coast, and had not been seen since. His clothes had been found on the beach, and the authorities had initially presumed that Tregelly had drowned after being swept out to sea by a strong current. However, several people who had known Tregelly had recently reported seeing him at a train station in Bristol.

Mrs Tregelly and her three children were heartbroken. If Tregelly had indeed drowned, it was a tragedy for his wife and family, and if the man had faked his own death, then it was no less heartbreaking for them. Police were keeping an open mind, as Lanyon Tregelly had owed a considerable amount of money to several banks. Furthermore, Tregelly was also suspected of being involved with a Devil-worshipping cult that was thought to have been responsible for a ritual killing of a vagrant. Henrietta trembled when she read that part. The article ended with a short description of Tregelly, and it seemed to fit Mr Glossop exactly – except for his lemon-dyed hair.

Henrietta lost no time in paying a visit to local policeman, PC Kinrade, and she told him about her suspicions regarding Mr Glossop. Kinrade and the sergeant of the local police station called upon Glossop at Runnymede Cottage, and the Cornishman strenuously denied that he was Tregelly and threatened to sue the policemen for slander. However, when a chief inspector visited the cottage with a search warrant, he found two letters from Tregelly's mistress in Cheshire, plus several documents with Lanyon Tregelly's signature upon them. Tregelly was taken back to Cornwall and put on trial for fraud. Lanyon Tregelly was sentenced to nine years hard labour at Dartmoor Prison. No evidence could be found to link him with the occult murder of the tramp though.

Not long after Tregelly's trial, a letter, written in animal blood, arrived at Henrietta Colquitt's home. It was allegedly from a member of the Devil-worshipping cult Tregelly had been involved with, and the author of the letter promised that he would cut out Henrietta's heart because she had led the police to 'Brother' Tregelly.

The Police branded the letter as a hoax, but not long afterwards, Henrietta Colquitt was awakened one night by a strange fluttering sound in her bedroom. She lit a bedside lamp – and saw a beheaded magpie flying crazily about. It bumped into the walls and furniture, smearing them with its blood, and the headless bird even flew into Henrietta's screaming face. How the bird had got into the room was never established, as all the windows were firmly closed.

This strange event was followed by a succession of other uncanny occurrences that ultimately drove Henrietta out of West Derby village.

THE ORMESHER GHOSTS

In May of 1956, a baffling but brutal double murder took place at Number 8 Asmall Lane in Ormskirk, where two elderly spinster sisters named Mary and Margaret Ormesher lived.

Mary Ormesher owned a sweets and tobacco shop in Ormskirk's Church Street, and she was a very sweet and inoffensive old lady, and had never had an enemy in the world. She and her sister were always helping people out; lending them money, giving the children a few extra free sweets and so on.

On Sunday 6 May 1956, at ten o'clock in the morning, Mrs Josephine Whitehouse, a woman who lived in a flat at the back of the Ormesher's shop in Church Street, called to the shop with a cup of tea as she usually did each morning, but was surprised to discover that the shop was still locked up. Mrs

Whitehouse therefore put on her coat and set off for the Ormesher sisters' house, a quarter of a mile away in Asmall Street.

Mrs Whitehouse called at the house but could get no answer, so she went next door to Number 6, where Mr Thomas Cummins lived. Mr Cummins and Mrs Whitehouse went into the alleyway and through the unlocked door of the back yard. One glance told him that something was amiss; the yard was littered with broken glass from an empty milk bottle and other debris, and the dustbin had also been overturned. Flecks of bright red blood spattered the whitewashed surfaces of the yard's brick walls.

Stepping their way carefully through the broken glass, Mr Cummins and Mrs Whitehouse then gazed through the kitchen window – and there they saw the bodies of Mary and Margaret Ormesher, lying on the kitchen floor, each in her own pool of blood. Mr Cummins pushed against the kitchen door and it opened. After studying the bodies from closer quarters for a moment or two to make sure that they were indeed dead, he ran off to fetch the police. The police station was only a hundred yards away at the end of the lane.

Near to the sisters' bodies the police found a leather attaché case which contained about fifty pounds in silver coins. Mrs Whitehouse confirmed that this was the case in which Mary Ormesher used to carry the takings home from the shop every Saturday night. Mrs Whitehouse told how she had always escorted Mary Ormesher to her home with the hundreds of pounds' worth of takings, but last night, which had been Saturday, Mrs Whitehouse had not been able to go with the old woman because she had been visiting friends in Southport. There were no notes in the attaché case and the bundles of paper money that had been kept secretly in an old grandfather clock had also been stolen. This discovery hinted that it was an inside job. Neighbours said that they had heard noises in the yard that night. A milk bottle being knocked over and a woman's voice crying, "Oh! Mr Cummins!"

A Mr Draper and a Mr Allison both claimed that they had heard the voices on the night of the crime. The two men were neighbours living on either side of the Ormeshers' house. The police investigated the baffling double murder but, despite all the clues, came to a dead end. Every person in Ormskirk over the age of sixteen was fingerprinted, and this amounted to a staggering twenty-four thousand inhabitants having their prints taken. However, frustratingly, no matches were found with any of the sets of fingerprints taken from the scene of the crime. Even men who had been on leave from the forces at the time of the murders were fingerprinted at their military locations around the country. Men in the neighbouring towns of Lathom, Burscough and Westhead were also fingerprinted, but still no matches were found.

The case is still unsolved to this day, but it is said that the ghosts of the murdered ladies have been seen on the anniversary of the heinous crime. One person who saw the spectres was Frank, from Halewood, who often visits Ormskirk to see his sister. He was brought up in the neighbourhood where the sisters were murdered, and remembers them both clearly.

One night, in May 1992, Frank was walking up Ormskirk's Church Street, when, on the other side of the road, he saw the ghosts of Mary and Margaret Ormesher standing close to the spot where their old shop had once stood. Frank did not feel at all frightened, and he crossed the road in amazement, but as he approached the figures, they vanished before his eyes. According to Frank, both of the apparitions had mournful expressions.

Many other people have reported seeing the ghosts of the murder victims, and perhaps the shades of the old women will continue to be seen in Ormskirk until their murders are finally solved.

A FLOWER CALLED LIVERPOOL

Flowers have always had a mystical association with the paranormal, dating back to ancient Egypt and the Bible. In the New Testament (Matthew 6: 28-30) Jesus says:

And why do you worry about clothes? See how the lilies of the field grow. They do not labour or spin. Yet I tell you that not even Solomon in all his splendour was dressed like one of these.

The lily Jesus was referring to was not the lily we know today, but the highly colourful flower A*nemone Coronaria*. A flowery magnolia bush also featured in a dream that turned out to be a turning point for the Swiss psychologist Carl Gustav Jung, and what's more, his dream was set in Liverpool. Here is what Jung said of his landmark dream:

I found myself in a dirty, sooty, city. It was night, and winter, and dark, and raining.

I was in Liverpool. With a number of Swiss – say, half a dozen – I walked through the dark streets. I had the feeling that we were coming from the harbour [Liverpool docks], and that the real city was actually up above, on the cliffs. We climbed up there. It reminded me of Basel, where the market is down below and then you go up through the Totengässchen ('Alley of the Dead'), which leads to a plateau above, and so to the Petersplatz and the Peterskirche. When we reached the plateau, we found a broad square dimly illuminated by street lights, into which many streets converged. The various quarters of the city were arranged radially around the square. In the centre was a round pool, and in the middle of it a small island. While everything round about was obscured by rain, fog, smoke, and dimly lit darkness, the little island blazed with sunlight. On it stood a single tree, a magnolia, in a shower of reddish blossoms. It was as though the tree stood in the sunlight and was at the same time the source of light. My companions commented on the abominable weather, and obviously did not see the tree. They spoke of another Swiss who was living in Liverpool, and expressed surprise that he should have settled here. I was carried away by the beauty of the flowering tree and the sunlit island, and thought, "I know very well why he has settled here". Then I awoke …

The dream represented my situation at the time. I can still see the greyish-yellow raincoats, glistening with the wetness of the rain. Everything was extremely unpleasant, black and opaque – just as I felt then. But I had had a vision of unearthly beauty, and that was why I was able to live at all. Liverpool is the 'pool of life'. The 'liver', according to an old view, is the seat of life – that which 'makes to live'.

This dream brought with it a sense of finality. I saw that here the goal had been revealed. One could not go beyond the centre. The centre is the goal, and everything is directed toward that centre. Through this dream I understood that the self is the principle and archetype of orientation and meaning. Therein lies its healing function. For me, this insight signified an approach to the centre and therefore to the goal. Out of it emerged a first inkling of my personal myth.

At the place where Jung saw the pool in his dream, such a pool actually existed, under the streets of Liverpool – beneath Mathew Street, where the Beatles were coming to prominence. The toilets of the Cavern often flooded because of the rising water levels from the subterranean pool, and ironically, a bust of Carl Jung proclaiming Liverpool to be the Pool of Life is mounted on the wall of the popular Flanagan's Apple traditional Irish pub in Mathew Street.

Victorians gave romantic significance to specific blossoms and flowers so that lovers could send one another secret messages. This secret language of flowers was used between courting couples, and also upon their wedding day, when they could spell out a romantic message by combining specific flowers. A red rose meant 'I love you,' a white rose symbolised purity and secrecy, a buttercup meant riches, forget-me-not stood for true love and so on. Many love affairs that ended in Victorian times often ended with the heartbroken partner sending a pink carnation to their lost love, which meant 'I will never forget you'.

In the world of the occult, there have been cases where unidentified flowers have appeared in séances. More often than not, these 'flowers of the afterlife', as some psychics like to refer to them, ultimately dematerialise after intruding into our dimension. Of course, some of these ectoplasmic flowers may have either been fakes, or simply rare flowers that are no longer blooming today.

In the early twentieth century there were once strange but beautiful purple flowers with checker-board patterns on their petals which were common in the wet meadows of Lancashire, but they became extinct through the use of agricultural practices such as draining, ploughing and the use of fertilisers. The same is sadly true of the Cheddar Pink (*Dianthus Gratianpolitanus*) and many other extremely rare British flowers. But the most mysterious of these vanished flowers is the one that was called 'Liverpool'. Here is the old tale of that flower.

In the 1870s, a young Liverpudlian, John O'Brien, was at large in both London, and the then second city of the Empire – Liverpool. At the bottom of Bold Street, at the junction of Hanover and Ranelagh Streets, Waterloo Place once existed, and here upon a sunny morning in the 1860s, fifty-nine-year-old David O'Brien was out walking with his fifteen-year-old son John, when he suffered what was probably a stroke. People gathered around as the Limerick-born man collapsed, and several bystanders offered words of reassurance to young John, who was obviously distressed at his father's sudden collapse.

Mr O'Brien was taken home, where his wife, six daughters and only son John gathered around his bedside. David O'Brien's condition was worsening by the minute, but he clung on to life for several days. A rag was wrapped around the front-door knocker, the curtains of the house were drawn shut, and the family prayed from dawn till dusk. A priest was summoned by Mrs O'Brien to administer the Last Rites, but before he arrived, Mr O'Brien requested a private meeting with his son John.

Pulling his son close to him, David gasped, "Never forget who you are, my son. You are descended from Brian Boru, High King of Ireland. Never let the O'Brien clan down. Stay honest and true."

"I promise you, father," sobbed John.

He clutched his father's hand and saw his last smile ... he had stopped breathing.

A wake after the funeral, attracting relatives who hadn't been in touch with the bereaved family for years. One of these relations was John's uncle Eamonn, who was the complete antithesis of his late brother David. Round and rosy-faced, Eamonn danced the jig whenever he could and knew the bawdiest jokes and most exciting yarns. Every amazing story ended with the phrase, "And that's as true as we're all sitting here."

He told the story about the poor Irish confidence trickster who earned a tidy sum by passing off an old mare who pulled a milk cart as the sister of the 1866 Grand National winner Salamander to a gullible rich dandy from London. Then Eamonn gave an animated recounting of the swindler cousin Barney Noonhan of Kildare, who accrued quite a fortune with his bogus make-money-overnight schemes. Mrs O'Brien noticed that her son was becoming captivated by Eamonn's tales of confidence tricksters and scoundrels, and she chastised her brother-in-law and told him to show some respect for her deceased husband.

Eamonn was used to criticism, which had no effect on him whatsoever, and he took lodgings close to the O'Briens' home, and started visiting regularly until he was finally sent packing by Mrs O'Brien. However, by the time that happened, John was completely enthralled by his uncle's talk of scams and clever frauds, and he ended up going to live with Eamonn. John soon started to associate with crooks and conmen, and he learned all of their tricks and their art. By 1874, John O'Brien was involved with a number of swindles and deceptions at various places about the city.

One day, John O'Brien was at a covered stall in an open-air market in the city, selling various innocent items of hardware – including an intriguing-looking box. Several people asked what the box was, and John casually stated that it was a 'universal copying apparatus' which was not for sale yet, as it required a licence from the Board of Trade. One affluent-looking gentleman seemed fascinated by the box, which was made of polished mahogany with several brass dials and a lever upon it. He repeatedly asked what the box did, and John finally looked about furtively, then fetched the box and pointed to the dials and the lever, explaining, "You simply feed in the paper to be copied into that slit, and you turn this dial to the numeral one, then you wind this other dial. You wait a minute – and no longer – and you turn the lever until the paper and the copy of the paper emerge from the slots at the other side of the box."

"Can it copy banknotes?" asked a shabbily-dressed man in a cloth cap, standing next to the gentleman, who was immediately alert to the money-making potential of the amazing machine.

John didn't answer.

"Well, can it?" the scruffy man asked.

"Well, yes, sir, it can, but that is illegal, and I am a law-abiding man," John told him, with a look of indignation.

The shabbily-dressed man took out a crinkled, dog-eared banknote, straightened it, and handed it to John. "Go ahead, copy this then. Let's see you do that."

"If I were caught doing that I'd be thrown into prison," John replied, and he put his hands around the box, ready to take it back to the shelf at the rear of the canvas-roofed stall.

The man in the cloth cap protested loudly and called John a liar.

"Universal copier! Hah!"

"Very well, give me that!" John fumed, and he thrust out his hand and took the banknote from the ragged sceptic.

"If you try to swap that money, or make out it's stuck in that thing, I'll smash your face in, I'm warning you," the shabby customer warned him.

The refined looking gentleman stood watching the proceedings without so much as a blink.

John carefully fed the banknote into the slit in the side of the box. He turned the gleaming brass dial indicator to the numeral one, and then wound the other dial, which sounded as if it was turning some spring-loaded mechanism. John then took out his fob watch and gazed at the dial.

"It takes one minute, as I explained," he said.

At the end of that minute, seven people had gathered at the stall to watch John O'Brien turn the lever of the universal copying apparatus. With each turn of the handle, two banknotes slid out from the slots on the other side of the box. The original creased banknote emerged fully, and on top of it was an identical but wet copy of the original. The man in the frayed clothes seemed stunned. The gentleman from the other end of society's social spectrum was equally startled. John O'Brien handed the original banknote to its owner, along with the brand new wet copy of it.

"Please destroy that copy, sir. I am not a counterfeiter," John said to the man in the dilapidated attire. The man inspected the wet banknote with a smile and asked John if he could carry out a few more demonstrations with the box – using his banknote again of course.

"It's all trickery, man!" said a man with a Scottish accent, stepping forward.

"It ain't trickery, mate, it's genuine," said the cloth-capped man, waving the copied banknote like a flag.

The Scotsman waved his hand at the man and produced a banknote from his own pocket. "Here, man, copy this then will ye?"

A Scottish banknote was slapped down on the stall counter.

"I can't, I'll get into trouble," John O'Brien told him. He turned to the man wearing the cap and said, beseechingly, "Sir, please destroy that copy!"

"Copy this and prove to me that this man here is not some accomplice!" demanded the Scotsman.

With great reluctance in his face and actions, John snatched the Bank of Scotland note and fed it into his box. He once again manipulated the box's dials and after a duration of one minute, he turned the lever with the utmost care, and out came two banknotes, one wet, one dry.

The Scotsman was visibly flabbergasted. He scrutinised the soaked paper of the banknote and shook his head. "But, but – how is it done?" he asked.

John went into a deep, obscure explanation about special inks and paper, and rollers, patented mechanisms, and ingenious German engraving chemicals.

"I don't want to know about all that!" interrupted the Scotsman. "Is the box for sale?"

"I can't sell it because the Royal Mint has to alter it so that it can't copy banknotes," John explained, a spellbound mob listening to every word by now. "The Governor of the Bank of England said I'll be a rich man if my patent is accepted."

"Damn the Governor! I'll buy that box off of ye!" said the Scotsman producing a wad of notes and eagerly reaching for the box.

The gentleman leaned forward and offered John O'Brien a vanilla-coloured card. Upon that card was this name and address: Henry Usher esq, Hanover Chambers, 19 Hanover Street, Liverpool.

"Bring that box and I will offer you more money than you could make in a lifetime," Mr Usher whispered.

"Sir, I cannot," said John O'Brien with some regret.

The man looked at the box and then reached for a money belt under his long coat. He watched the crowd suspiciously, then produced over a hundred pounds and clenched it in his fist. The fist was thrust out to John O'Brien, who was waving away the Scotsman's handful of money. The crowd was growing, and suddenly, a rogue who had been watching the proceedings vaulted over the stall counter and seized the money-copying box. Everybody gasped. Then a man slammed the silver ornate handle of a walking cane down on the thief's head. The criminal's legs buckled beneath him. The situation was rapidly getting out of hand, and a policeman was sure to investigate the scrum soon. John quickly picked up the box and looked around at the faces of the mob, trembling with apprehension.

"Take the money, man!" shrieked the exasperated Usher, as he stuffed the banknotes into John O'Brien's jacket pocket.

John threw his hand up to his face, apparently terrified.

"Please, sir, don't use it to copy money, I beseech you!"

"You have my word," said Henry Usher with undisguised glee, as he snatched the mahogany box and went to hail a hansom cab.

John O'Brien, meanwhile, swiftly closed the stall and hurried home to share Usher's money with his two accomplices – the man in the cap and the Scotsman! The box of course, could copy nothing. The trick had been performed with rubber rollers and the box had already been supplied with two banknotes – one English, the other of a Scottish denomination. Mr Usher's greed and imagination had done the rest.

The scams continued, and sometimes the hapless victims caught up with O'Brien and gave him a severe beating. In fact, so notorious did he become, that it was no longer safe for him to operate in Liverpool.

In 1875, John O'Brien found himself waiting at Liverpool Docks, where he was due to sail to Australia on the SS Great Britain. At the dockside, a beautiful young flower-seller approached him, and he was immediately taken by her good looks. She carried a tray of heather – and one single flower that John had never seen before. The girl picked up the bloom from her tray and offered it to him.

"That's a strange flower," John said, receiving it in his outstretched palm.

At first he thought it was some kind of unusual rose, but the fiery red petals radiated out from a royal blue disc that was speckled with tiny white tubular stamens, that formed a letter X. The leaves on the exotic flower's stem were identical to those of the shamrock, and its scent was sweet and uplifting.

The flower girl asked for no money in return. She said the name of the flower was 'Liverpool'. The white cross in the centre of the flower head symbolised St Andrew's cross, the emblem of Scotland, the vivid red petals stood for the red dragon – the ancient symbol of the Welsh, and the shamrock leaves stood for Ireland. The scent was reminiscent of the red rose, which represented England. Over time, the people of England, Ireland, Scotland and Wales had come to live together in Liverpool.

John O'Brien felt so sad when the girl told him this. Here he stood, about to abandon the city he loved because of his dishonest ways, despite the fact that he had promised his dying father that he would pursue a life of honesty. As John gazed pensively at the flower, the flower girl suddenly looked at him meaningfully and said, "Stay honest and true".

John recoiled in shock. Was she a mind reader? How on earth could she have known that they were his father's last words. The SS *Great Britain* was ready to sail, and John was forced forward by the surging crowds making their way to the ship's gangways. The flower girl was swallowed up by the crowds at the quayside. Three-hundred and eighty-seven passengers boarded the ship, among them John O'Brien, with his assumed name and his small packing case.

Sixty-seven days later, the SS *Great Britain* docked at Melbourne. In Australia, John perpetrated a few scams, but ironically, fell for one himself. A 'gold prospector' led him into the desert to show him a series of cryptic symbols carved into a rock that were said to have been made by a long-missing explorer named Leichardt. The prospector claimed that if the symbols were decoded they would lead to a fabled gold mine. Once they were far away from civilisation, that same prospector robbed John O'Brien at gunpoint, and left him to die in the desert.

For five days, John crawled along in the blistering sun, until he decided that he couldn't continue. He repeatedly reached into his pockets, hoping against hope that he would find something to eat. He did not find any food, but he did find something that gave him powerful inspiration to go on living for as long as possible. It was the flower – Liverpool – slightly crumpled, but still smelling as sweet as it had on the Liverpool Docks. He could instantly see his beloved city in his mind's eye, and remembered what his father had said about the O'Brien clan: "Never forget who you are, my son. You are descended from Brian Boru, High King of Ireland. Never let the O'Brien clan down. Stay honest and true."

John O'Brien somehow struggled to his feet and surveyed the unending, featureless desert that stretched before him. He recalled the epic tales of his ancestor Boru, and how he had fought the invading Vikings. As John trudged on through the fiery desert hell, he saw countless mirages, which appeared, then melted away on the wobbling, fluctuating horizon.

For mile after mile he continued, until he suddenly spied a man walking towards him. The figure undulated, quivered, became elongated, then vanished, only to reappear time and time again. It was getting closer, and its arms were outstretched towards him. Then John realised, to his great surprise, that it was his dear father, dressed in a flowing white robe.

"Father!" he cried, staggering towards the tantalising apparition, but when he was just thirty feet away from it, the figure vanished. John was about to cry out in despair, when he suddenly noticed that the arid desert had given way to greenery. At first, he believed that it too was a mirage, but he walked on anyway, and sweet floral scents wafted towards him on the desert air. The greenery turned out to be a eucalyptus forest; John had finally reached the edge of the desert. He was picked up there by a group of British soldiers who were surveying in the area and was immediately taken to hospital.

John O'Brien returned to Liverpool, and decided to carry out honest work to make a living. Throughout his life, he showed many people the pressed flower that had kept him going in the desert, but no one ever identified its genus. It remained as mysterious as the flower seller who had given John the bloom, and who was never seen again on the streets of Liverpool.

SIMILAR TITLES
Published by The Bluecoat Press

HAUNTED LIVERPOOL 1	Tom Slemen	£5.99
HAUNTED LIVERPOOL 2	Tom Slemen	£5.99
HAUNTED LIVERPOOL 3	Tom Slemen	£5.99
HAUNTED LIVERPOOL 4	Tom Slemen	£5.99
HAUNTED LIVERPOOL 5	Tom Slemen	£5.99
HAUNTED LIVERPOOL 6	Tom Slemen	£5.99
HAUNTED LIVERPOOL 7	Tom Slemen	£5.99
HAUNTED LIVERPOOL AUDIO BOOK read by	Tom Slemen	£8.99
HAUNTED WIRRAL	Tom Slemen	£5.99
WICKED LIVERPOOL	Tom Slemen	£5.99
MYSTERIES	Tom Slemen	£5.99
TOM SLEMEN'S MYSTERIOUS WORLD	Tom Slemen	£5.99
A DIFFERENT SKY (UFOs IN MERSEYSIDE)	Tony Eccles	£5.99

Available from all good bookshops
For a free stocklist contact
The Bluecoat Press, 45 Bluecoat Chambers, School Lane, Liverpool L1 3BX
Telephone 0151 707 2390

If you have had a paranormal encounter,
or a supernatural experience of any sort,
please drop a line to: Tom Slemen c/o The Bluecoat Press.

All correspondence will be answered.